Artist: Francine Auger

Agnes Macphail, 1890-1954.

Rachel Wyatt

Rachel Wyatt was born in Yorkshire, England but has been a Canadian citizen since 1957. Early in her career she wrote features for various magazines and newspapers. She has had over one hundred radio dramas commissioned and produced by the CBC and thirty by the BBC. Her stage plays have been produced in theatres in British Columbia, Alberta, Manitoba, Ontario, and Nova Scotia as well as in Philadelphia, U.S.A. and London, England. She also has written scripts and short features for television.

Wyatt has published five novels and one collection of short fiction. Her most recent books are *Mona Lisa Smiled a Little* (Oolichan, 1999), *The Day Marlene Dietrich Died* (Oolichan, 1996), and a play based on Adele Wiseman's novel, *Crackpot* (Playwrights Canada Press, 1995).

She has given readings and lectures at literary festivals and universities in Europe, Australia, and across Canada. For several summers, she taught English to Inuit teachers in the Arctic.

Rachel Wyatt has just retired as Program Director, Writing, at the Banff Centre for the Arts. She held that position from 1991-1999. She was Associate Director from 1987 to 1991. She was also Director of the Banff Radio Drama Workshop from 1989 to 1996.

Rachel now lives in Victoria with her husband, Alan Wyatt.

Agnes Macphail

Canadian Cataloguing in Publication Data

Wyatt, Rachel, 1929-

   Agnes Macphail : champion of the underdog

   (The Quest Library ; 5)
   Includes bibliographical references and index.

   ISBN 0-9683601-5-7

   1. Macphail, Agnes Campbell, 1890-1954. 2. Women legislators – Canada – Biography. 3. Feminists – Canada – Biography. 4. Reformers – Canada – Biography. 5. Women legislators – Ontario – Biography. I. Title. II. Series.

FC541.M27W92 2000   328.71'092   C00-940653-0
F1034.W92 2000

Legal Deposit: Second quarter 2000
National Library of Canada
Bibliothèque nationale du Québec

XYZ Publishing acknowledges the support of The Quest Library project by the Canadian Studies Program and the Book Publishing Industry Development Program (BPIDP) of the Department of Canadian Heritage. The opinions expressed do not necessarily reflect the views of the Government of Canada.

The publishers further acknowledge the financial support our publishing program receives from The Canada Council for the Arts, the ministère de la Culture et des Communications du Québec, and the Société de développement des entreprises culturelles.

Chronology: Lynne Bowen
Layout: Édiscript enr.
Photo researcher: Anne Phillips
Cover design: Zirval Design
Cover illustration: Francine Auger

Printed and bound in Canada

XYZ Publishing   Distributed by: General Distribution Services
1781 Saint Hubert Street   325 Humber College Boulevard
Montreal, Quebec H2L 3Z1   Toronto, Ontario M9W 7C3
Tel: (514) 525-2170   Tel: (416) 213-1919
Fax: (514) 525-7537   Fax: (416) 213-1917
E-mail: xyzed@mlink.net   E-mail: customer.service@emailgw.genpub.com

MACPHAIL

Agnes

CHAMPION OF THE UNDERDOG

XYZ
Publishing

Contents

The Normal School, Stratford.
Agnes Macphail learned her teaching skills at this school
and went on to become its most celebrated graduate.

1

Good morning, Miss Macphail

Good morning, children!

Agnes was fourteen years old, running home from school, waving a certificate to say she had passed the high school entrance exam. This was it, the passport to a teaching career, to independence. She pictured herself going into a classroom on a September day in a few years' time and greeting her pupils.

It was a warm Ontario afternoon, the corn was coming up, the apple and peach trees were full of still-unripe fruit. Agnes ran first to tell the good news to her friends and neighbours, the Olivers. Then she went on to share her triumph with her Grandmother Campbell.

"And I'll be going to high school in September!"

Her grandmother congratulated her and then said something that Agnes never forgot. "Remember, when you get on in life, you must always try to help those not as fortunate as you."

The happy girl went on home to the farmhouse her family had moved into two years before, in the little town of Ceylon in Proton Township. She couldn't wait to see the proud look on her parents' faces when she told them of her achievement and her plans. But the look on their faces was not what she expected. They were proud, of course, but they had other ideas for her future.

"You're grown up now, dear," her mother said. "And we need you here to help on the farm, in the house."

Her father explained to her that as his job took him away sometimes, they couldn't manage without her. Eventually she would marry and have a family and a farm of her own.

She saw it, that picture of her future, as a black shadow falling over all her hopes. One moment she had been excited and looking forward to three more years of education and a career, and the next all she could see was the hard labour of farm work for ever and ever, doing repetitive chores day in and day out till she was as old as Grandma Campbell.

At least, unlike her younger sisters, Gertha and Lilly, and because she had nagged her father, she was allowed to help with the cows and horses. It wasn't to be all "women's work," polishing and scrubbing and ironing. Her parents' word was law, but the girl didn't give up easily; she came from a line of strong-minded Scottish immigrants.

Her ancestors had left one place where the climate was hard and the work difficult and had come to another where the climate was worse and their lives no easier. But the Campbells and MacPhails had land of their own; they were independent, proud people, and Agnes was proud to be one of them.

∞

One day in a schoolroom in Scotland many decades before, a young boy sat down at his desk and wrote:

Dear Teacher, In a few years I will go to America where there are no landlords and no rent and no queen. I will get a house of my own there and a farm, maybe two farms. I will have a home of my own and a farm before I am thirty years old, and a wife too.

This letter was an entry in a competition to describe a plan for the future, and the boy won a steel pen for it. Several years later, he emigrated to Canada and made his plan come true. He was John Campbell, Agnes's grandfather.

∞

When her grandmother told her stories of life in Scotland, she imitated the voice of the Presbyterian preacher who called the Campbells "sinners" because they grew potatoes. "Potatoes are the devil's tubers," the minister warned from his pulpit. "They will bring down sickness upon us all. Palsy and scurvy and leprosy will spread among us like a plague if you eat these things."

He refused to baptize any more of the Campbell children, and so, although the family was making a good living selling "devil's tubers" to the soldiers stationed nearby, young John knew it was time to leave.

"And when your grandfather set sail for the New World, he brought me with him as his bride," Grandmother Campbell said.

Agnes loved these tales, but she shed tears when Jean Campbell told of their hardships on the journey across the Atlantic. She and John had to work their passage on a sailing ship, the *Heather Bell*. Contrary winds slowed the boat down, and the journey from England to Canada took ten weeks. Their little baby died on the way.

By 1855, after working at many jobs in the new country and saving their money, the young couple was able to buy a piece of land with a house on it. They settled on the fourteenth concession in Proton Township, Grey County.

These family stories kept Agnes going as she did her chores, biding her time until the miracle would happen and her wish to go to high school would come true. The days were long and full and tiring. But in the evenings when the work was done and the lamps were reflecting their light on the polished furniture, neighbours and relatives gathered by the fire to sit and talk.

"We're not getting a fair price for the corn."

"If the frost comes too soon, we're ruined."

"We'll never afford that new plough."

As Agnes quietly took all this in, she thought about how the farmers might make their lives easier. Little did she know that she would spend most of her life fighting on their behalf.

When the family was alone, Dougald MacPhail would conjure up a picture of rolling Scottish hillsides for his daughters.

"My grandfather," he told them, "was a shepherd. He guarded sheep for a Scottish laird. Hundreds of them all over the glen. He and his dog would make sure the new lambs were safe in spring. When he was a boy, my dad many a time had to go out and dig a way through the snow to save the newborns."

Dougald, who was a good storyteller, always made much of the next part of his tale. "And when the MacPhails came to Canada and my dad looked for land of his own, where did he settle but almost next door to the Campbells. So that," he would say with a glance at his wife, "is how we all come to be here, sitting by this fire now."

Grey County was part good farming country, suitable for growing wheat and for raising cattle, and part swampy and stony ground. The work of clearing and tilling the soil was hard and wearisome, but the Campbells and MacPhails who moved there were determined to make a living in their chosen country.

∞

Grandmother MacPhail had a different story to tell about her beginnings. When she was a girl, she and her family had walked the hundred miles across Ontario, from Hamilton to Grey County, carrying their belongings, to find a place to farm. When she was only twelve her mother died, and she had to care for the new baby as well as the other children. "I would carry the maple sugar on my back twenty miles to Mount Forest to sell, and sometimes it melted in the heat. And then there was trouble."

Her son, Dougald, married Henrietta, daughter of John and Jean Campbell, in 1889. They took over a nearby farm with a barn and a log house, and on March 24th the following year their first child was born and christened "Agnes."

The land was poor and the log house cold in winter. Etta MacPhail kept the cabin sparkling clean, made meals for the workers, and had little time for holidays. She was not a lighthearted woman. She expected Agnes and her sisters, Gertha and Lilly, to pick themselves up when they fell and to carry on without crying. If Christmas Day chanced to fall on a Monday, the sheets had to be washed just the same.

"For a long time," Agnes said later, "I thought Santa Claus didn't know my address."

Agnes's father never did manage to build the better house on that property as he'd promised his wife when they married. Instead, he took a new job. A charming, well-spoken man, he became an auctioneer, selling cattle at the local markets. Agnes was twelve when the MacPhails moved to a farm near Ceylon. The new house was made of brick; it was larger, more comfortable, and it could be heated in winter, all the way through.

While she was looking after the cattle or scrubbing the floor or rubbing the sheets against a washboard or making bread, Agnes was thinking of ways to get to high school. She knew she had it in her to be someone, to do something, to help others as her Grandmother Campbell told her she should. She wanted a husband and children, but she saw no reason why being a woman should prevent her from having a career as well.

"Does this thing never end in a woman being a person and making a contribution in addition to having children?" she asked out loud.

∞

Life on the farm went on. The seasons came and went. Agnes helped to pick and preserve fruit and make pickles and gather eggs and bake. In winter she trekked out to the barn to feed the animals. In her spare time, she read the stories of G.D. Roberts and Dickens and Stevenson. On some winter evenings, all the young people round about would pile into a sleigh and go off to a nearby farm or hall and dance to music played by a couple of fiddlers.

When she heard her parents talking over the high price of goods and the low price they got for their produce or the neighbours complaining about the horrors of the tariff system, she would murmur, "If I went to high school, I could get a job and earn money. If I went to high school, I could maybe do something about the tariff system."

Agnes was not cut out to be a silent martyr.

When Dougald and Henrietta told the old stories of their parents and the way they had overcome such hardships to get their own land, Agnes took heart. It would happen. It would come about. Finally, after two years, her parents caved in, and the happy day came when Dougald said to his daughter, "Very well, but we'll find you a good high school, the best."

He made enquiries and discovered that the school in Owen Sound had an excellent reputation. Agnes began to sew and to pack. The family couldn't afford many new clothes, but she would have gladly gone off to Owen Sound in her old, worn working skirt.

When she said goodbye to her mother and sisters and Dougald took her and her trunk in the trap to the station, her excitement at the prospect of her new life overcame her sadness at leaving home for the first time.

I am on my way. I am on my way, she said to herself to the beat of the wheels on the thirty-mile train journey to Owen Sound. Trains were slow then and the price of a ticket costly. Agnes knew she could only go home for major holidays, but even that didn't matter now.

In choosing a school for his daughter, Dougald MacPhail hadn't reckoned with the attitude of the town girls to a young woman from the farm.

"Look at her clothes," the local girls said, turning up their noses. "Another hayseed."

Grandmother Campbell had told Agnes she should never look down on anyone, whatever their race or station in life, and here were these girls despising the people Agnes had grown up with and whom she knew to be the best in the world.

"And where do you think your milk and eggs come from?" she retorted.

To her, the town girls seemed flighty, only interested in clothes and unable to carry on real conversation. There were days when she was homesick and when she wondered whether she should have stayed in Ceylon after all and followed the path her parents had mapped out for her, married some young farmer and reared a family.

There was no dancing and no social events were organized to bring the young people of the town together. The annual Promenade was exactly that. The boys and girls promenaded round in pairs like animals going into the ark.

Things began to look up when Agnes joined the Literary Society. She took part in debates and soon found she was ahead of the others when it came to making a reasoned argument.

The principal of the school was a good teacher, although he was inclined to be overbearing and to pick on the weak students. But Agnes wasn't afraid to answer back even then.

As Mr. Murray went past her desk one day, he tripped over her feet.

"Now Miss Macphail," he said. "I wonder why I should fall over your feet?"

"Probably because your own are so big," Agnes replied.

The others gasped, expecting some angry response from the teacher. But he had come to like Agnes and her forthright ways and only smiled. Besides, she was one of his best students.

When one of the town girls came to her for help with her homework, Agnes said, "I guess I thought the possession of a bathtub meant the possession of a brain." But she helped the other student with her math, and by now all the students knew that the girl from the farm was smarter than most of them.

At eighteen, Agnes passed the junior matriculation examination and was ready to go on to Normal School to train to be a teacher.

Henrietta and Dougald, remembering her not-so-quiet persistence last time around, got the money together for her fees. She could go, but she must live with her uncle while she was in Stratford.

The Campbell family, rejected long ago in Scotland by the Presbyterians, had joined the Church of the Latter-day Saints. Her uncle was a religious man and expected his young niece to follow the rules. Agnes admired the Church and all it stood for except for one thing: dancing was forbidden. Whether she surreptitiously went out to dance with her fellow students or managed to keep her feet still for a year, at least she did all the work required at Normal School, passed the examination, and was ready to take up a post as an apprentice teacher.

On the September day when she walked into her first schoolroom at Gowanlocks, Agnes was nervous but very happy. She was a teacher at last and she would show her parents that their investment in her was worthwhile. She was an independent woman with a salary of five hundred dollars a year.

She smiled at the boys and girls, most of them from farm families, and wanted for them all a good and useful life. They looked at their new young teacher and said, "Good morning, Miss Macphail."

The rural schoolteacher, 1921.
She taught by day and danced the night away.

2

Finding Her Voice

S itting in his office in Toronto one morning, a middle-aged man was reading an indignant letter from a young schoolteacher:

In response to the letter in your paper in which your correspondent complained of the living conditions in rural homes, I would like to say that during my time as a teacher, I have stayed with many farm families and found them without exception to be comfortable, clean, and the people very hospitable.

There was more in the letter about the hard and necessary and often unappreciated work done by farmers, and as the man read, he saw that here was someone who might speak out clearly on behalf of the farming community.

The man was the editor of the *Farmers' Sun*, the journal of the United Farmers of Ontario, and the letter writer was Agnes Macphail.

∞

Agnes enjoyed her first weeks in the classroom. She was young and lively, and the students were responsive to her. She taught them arithmetic and heard them recite, "Up the airy mountain, Down the rushy glen, We daren't go a-hunting, For fear of little men."

Most of the textbooks were British and had little to do with rural life in Canada, but Agnes made sure that her class knew what was going on in the world around them.

The ties to the old country were still strong. The black-draped photograph of the late King Edward was taken down and the newly crowned King George V and Queen Mary gazed sternly from the wall. The day began with the singing of the national anthem.

When royalty came to visit, huge crowds turned out to cheer. One farmer's son said, "I knew the Royal Family were next only to God because when the Prince of Wales came to town my dad let us take a day off in harvest-time to watch him pass by."

Agnes went home to Ceylon at Thanksgiving full of stories about her pupils and the happy family she was living with, and she had ninety dollars burning a hole in her purse. It was her first earned money. She stopped off in town to buy gifts for her parents and sisters, and a new hat for herself.

"I'm home," she said, as her sisters came to greet her at the door of the farmhouse. She waited till evening, when the chores were done and the family was gathered by the fire, to hand the gifts round and to show off her new hat. She stood back, expecting thanks and admiration.

There was a moment of silence.

"How could you throw your money about like this?" her mother demanded.

Her father gave her one of those half-sad, half-angry looks that told her she had been foolish.

"You still have to pay back the fees for Normal School so that Lilly can go."

The fire seemed to lose its warmth and the glow of her first day home was gone – but only until one of the local boys, knowing Aggie to be home, came by and invited her to a dance.

∽

She had a happy year at Gowanlocks, but Normal School graduates were advised to resign at the end of their first year to make way for other new teachers. By this method, the school board could choose either to advertise for a new teacher or to re-hire the same one.

It was a blow to Agnes when the Gowanlocks board hired someone else. They had wanted her to stay but mistakenly took her resignation to mean she wasn't happy there.

∽

"Come and listen to this, Aggie."

She moved on to a school in Kinloss and lodged with Mr. and Mrs. Sam Braden, who owned two stores. When the farmers came to buy their seed and their groceries, they would stay and chat to Sam. At first Agnes sat on the steps and listened, but soon she began to join in.

"The tariffs are killing us," they said.

"I'll never be able to buy another horse."

If the farmers were slow to organize, they were never slow to talk.

"We've got to have Free Trade."

"The manufacturers are getting it all their own way as usual."

"And where does that leave us?"

"They say if they lower the tariffs we'll become one more State in the Union."

"Read the *Globe*," Sam Braden advised Agnes. "And read the *Mail and Empire*. That way you'll get the Liberal point of view and the Conservative as well. And then you can make up your own mind."

On Election Day in 1911, the news came over the telegraph wire: Sir Wilfrid Laurier, the Liberal Prime Minister, had been defeated. The Conservatives were jubilant, but the farmers who gathered in Sam's store that day were quiet. They'd lost their only support. Their dejection struck the young teacher to the core. What could be done? What could she do?

She was doing more than joining in political discussions, she was teaching all day and dancing many a night. She couldn't resist the call of the music and often got home at daybreak just in time to change and go on to the school to face her pupils. By the end of the school year, she was exhausted.

∞

"Three cheers for Miss Macphail."

The students and their parents gave a farewell party for the popular teacher. They showered her with rose petals, made speeches to her, and gave her gifts. She went back to Ceylon honoured, pleased with her success in the classroom – and ill.

"This teaching is too much for you," her mother said when her daughter arrived home pale and thin and too tired to get up, let alone go dancing.

She grew worse and the doctor was sent for.

"What you have," he pronounced, "is an inward goitre."

"I know you can operate for that," Agnes said. "Operate on me."

"It's just too dangerous, my dear," the doctor answered. Two of his patients had died after the same operation, and he wasn't going to risk it on another.

As he walked out of her room, Agnes heard the doctor tell her mother that she would never be able to work again.

"No," she shouted. "No. I'm not going to sit by the fire and knit for the rest of my life."

Her sisters brought her food and tried to cheer her up. She lay back on her bed in despair. Never work again! Was she now, after being given a glimpse of life, of being her own woman, to be the semi-invalid who could only do light work and must sit by the fire, knitting? It was a black hour. And the family, creeping around her, trying to comfort her, could do nothing to help.

But she was Agnes Macphail. She wasn't about to lie down and play dead for the rest of her life at the age of twenty-three.

When she felt a little better, she went to stay with her aunt and uncle in Alberta. Her parents were reluctant to let her go, but once more she got her own way.

"I'll get a part-time job to pay for my keep," she told them, and off she went.

And this time the beat of train wheels as she travelled across the country was saying, *I will work again. I will work again.* She looked out at the huge fields planted with wheat, the giant grain elevators beside the stations. Here was farming on a truly grand scale.

∞

Once in Alberta, Agnes found a six-month teaching job. Rather than making her better, the move almost finished her off. The living conditions were harsher than in Ontario. The wind seemed to blow right through the doors and windows of the houses. The log cabin at its worst hadn't been as cold as this.

Because their homes were some distance away, the children rode ponies to school and Agnes rode one of her uncle's horses. One October day the children in her class were restless, wanting to go home.

"There's going to be a storm," they told her, but Agnes thought they were playing tricks on her and she kept right on teaching.

Suddenly a strong wind began to blow snow across the windows and to beat at the walls. An anxious father came with a wagon to take most of the children home. Agnes and some other students lived in the other direction.

"Stay close to Mary," the man told Agnes. "Or you'll be lost."

It was a freezing, blinding ride to the farmhouse where the girl lived. Agnes had no choice but to spend the night there, and it was a night she never forgot.

"The wind howled and shrieked," she wrote later, "and blew snow half way across the main room of the house as I sat and shivered in a chair. One of the family said, 'Do you never have storms in Ontario?' 'Oh yes,' I said, 'We have bad storms but then we have houses too!'"

She realized at once that it was a rude way to talk to her host, but as often happened, her sharp tongue got the better of her.

And that was it for the West as far as Agnes was concerned. She resigned and returned to Ontario to complete her apprenticeship in a school in Boothville, Grey County, filling in for a sick teacher. She never knew whether she had suffered from "inward goitre" or what it was that had made her so ill. She was simply delighted to know that all her old energy had returned.

∽

She took her first job as a qualified member of the profession at Pegg's school near Sharon in East Gwillimbury Township. The students liked her, their parents liked her. She was soon known all over town as "Mac."

Being closer to Toronto, Sharon had more urban amenities; there were a few cars on the roads and better stores but not much money to spare.

When the school needed decorating, Agnes and her students raised part of the funds towards it. They had window boxes made to brighten up the outside. She encouraged the start of a school magazine and introduced the students to current affairs by picking a topic from the daily papers for discussion. Left to themselves, she said, the children would pick only the horror stories.

Agnes's own political feelings were developing and she was beginning to think that there might be more in her future than being a country schoolteacher. But a long time later she wrote, "... afterwards when public criticism of me was severe, I wondered why I left off teaching in the splendid communities I have described."

∞

She couldn't help becoming involved in the problems of the people she knew best, the farmers. She read all she could about co-operative systems and ways of bringing farm communities together to lobby for better treatment. In those days, a large part of the population lived in rural areas, either farming, or supplying the farmers and their families with the goods they needed.

When she received the letter from the editor of the *Farmers' Sun*, Agnes was surprised. She hadn't expected a reply. As she read it, she understood that he was inviting her, a woman, to join a political organization, the United Farmers of Ontario. As a rural teacher she was eligible to be a member. She could go to their meetings and at last she would have a chance to speak out for the men and women who were getting a raw deal.

Her first public speech lasted ten minutes. Standing up nervously at a meeting of the United Farmers, she read out her title, "Why Farmers Should Organize." She looked at the men and women sitting on the hard chairs in the hall and gathered courage to go on. "You cannot," she said, "expect others to solve your problems. Many of those 'others' are making money that should be coming to you. They are not going to look after your interests."

But farmers were busy coping with the day-to-day running of their farms and few would come forward.

Later she said, "Farmers in that day were too reluctant to get up on their feet and talk in their own defence."

☙

Now once again Agnes was stretching herself to the limit. She was teaching by day, attending meetings in the evenings and on weekends, and still finding time to dance now and then, too.

One winter evening, after making a speech away from home, she became suddenly ill with fever and chills and had to stay in bed. She sent reassuring messages to her parents, but her father sensed that something serious was wrong. He called the local doctor and found out the truth. She had smallpox! And there she was, kept in quarantine for several weeks in the house where she had only intended to spend the night. Her kind hosts made room for her and her nurse. The days went very slowly for Agnes, but she used the time to think of future plans and to read.

At this time, the movement to get the vote for women was becoming louder and more widespread. In England, women were chaining themselves to railings, marching, being arrested. In jail, on hunger strikes, they suffered the indignity of forced feeding, of having men stuff a tube down their throats in order to keep them alive.

In Toronto, Dr. Emily Stowe had started the Women's Literary Club, Canada's first suffrage group. Her daughter, Ann Augusta Stowe-Gullen, carried on as president of the Dominion Women's Enfranchisement Association when her mother died. In Canada the revolution was quieter than in England, but it was led by a number of persistent women. Nothing so far had been achieved. Women had no vote and were barred from entering Parliament. Dr. Stowe was not allowed to go to medical school in Canada and had to go to the States to study. When she returned home, she wasn't allowed to practise medicine for some years.

Becoming aware of all this did nothing for Agnes's blood pressure, but it made her determined to add her voice to those crying out for equality.

When she was well, she took up her busy life again. At a meeting with the federal finance minister, when he was trying to tell the farmers that the system was good for them, she stood up to speak in their defence.

"The protective tariffs are keeping the farmers in a similar state of subjection as that in which the Hudson's Bay Company used to keep the aboriginal peoples," she said, referring to the fur trade and the way in which the hunters were forced to buy goods from Hudson's Bay stores in return for their furs.

The Minister was astounded to hear a woman speak out in this way. But others in the audience knew Agnes by now, and before long her name was being spoken in the rural areas as someone who might stand for Parliament. A few years before, this would have been unthinkable. The war in Europe had changed the attitude of the lawmakers and reluctantly they were admitting women into their world.

Before the First World War, politicians had turned down every request of women's groups to allow them to vote or to allow them to enter Parliament. The men had all kinds of excuses: It would weaken family life if women took office; women would vote frivolously; it was best for women to be guided by men. At last, in 1917, women in Ontario were given the vote in provincial elections. And in that year two women were elected to the Alberta legislature. Women whose next of kin were fighting in the war were given a vote in the federal election. Finally, the government granted the right to vote federally to all women who already had a vote in their provinces.

A year after the war ended, the heavy doors of the House of Commons were opened to the opposite sex. Women could, if they chose, stand for Parliament.

There was a provincial election in Ontario, and Agnes Macphail was invited to the nomination meetings as a speaker. Her views and her voice were a valuable asset to the farmers' cause.

To their surprise, and to everyone else's, the United Farmers of Ontario won forty-four seats at Queen's Park, Toronto. They were in power. But they were not in the usual sense a political party. They were "united" in their views but they voted independently.

Agnes felt the excitement of this victory. If farmers could win in Ontario, what could they not do across the country?

∽

Towards the end of the school year, she had a dream: "I saw my lovely grandmother as a miniature, being dragged along by the hand of a normal-sized woman; the little lady was protesting that she couldn't go on so fast even when she tried her best. Finally, after what seemed a long walk, she turned and looked over her shoulder and said, 'Aggie, come and take care of me.'"

Agnes took this dream at its face value; her grandmother was frail and needed her. But did it really mean that Agnes the teacher now needed to look after the political Agnes who was making her way into public life?

She resigned from her job and went to look after her beloved Grandmother Campbell.

Once back in Proton, she continued to make speeches. At a local picnic, when the Conservative MP upset the farmers by criticizing their methods, Agnes said, "You know nothing at all of the way farmers live, of their work, and their problems." The farmers cheered.

Newspapers were taking note of this woman who spoke so well. She was talked of in places like Sam Braden's store. She was saying all the right things and she was making people sit up and listen. A group of people put her name forward as a nominee for the South-East Grey constituency in the forthcoming federal election.

Agnes lay low. She listened to the talk but had the sense not to push herself forward. She looked after her grandmother, she helped around the farm at home, and she waited.

Her parents were worried. Up to now, their clever daughter had been treated with kindness, with respect and admiration. Dougald and Etta MacPhail perhaps understood better than she did the hostility that a woman might encounter in Ottawa. Probably the only woman in that male world. A woman from a farm community!

The set-up of the nomination meeting would have daunted anyone. There were eleven would-be candidates – ten men and Agnes. Each of them had to speak and say what he or she would do on behalf of the people. When it was Agnes's turn, she looked out at the crowd and saw her sisters, Gertha and Lilly, their husbands, her friends the Olivers, and many supporters from the farming communities around.

The voting took all the long afternoon. The large group of supporters from Proton Township made all the difference. Agnes Macphail was chosen out of the eleven contestants to stand as the United Farmers of Ontario candidate in the next federal election.

This in itself was a huge step forward for women. For Agnes it meant the possibility of working for her own people, the men and women who worked the land.

But first she had to get elected.

3

Speaking for the Farmers

"**A** woman! Are there no men in South-East Grey?"
The old farmer's question was echoed in many
of the meeting places in the townships and villages.
What would the rest of the country think of them if
they sent a woman to Parliament, supposing of
course that the woman could win, which was totally
unlikely!

The local executive of the United Farmers listened to the talk and cravenly called another nomination meeting so that another vote could be taken. The
same ten men were there to put their names forward
and make the same speeches.

"Will you stand down, Miss Macphail?" the chairman asked.

The House that became a battleground
and a "home" for Agnes Macphail

Agnes, feeling a little like Joan of Arc facing her accusers, looked around the hall. There again were her sisters Gertha and Lilly and their husbands, her friends the Olivers, and many others who had given her their support, all waiting for her answer. She was being asked to stand aside to make way for a "better" choice: a man.

It would have been easy in that moment to stand aside and let them have their way. But what would Emily Stowe have said? Or the whole army of women who had been working for decades to make this happen? What would her Grandmother Campbell say? And how would she be able to look at herself in the mirror ever again if she let this great chance slip away?

"I won fair and square," she said, and stood her ground.

Grumbling, the ten men gave in. All she had to do now was prove to them that she could win a seat and represent them in the House of Commons. She set out to make speeches to voters in all the corners of Grey County.

Always thrifty, careful with the meagre party funds, Agnes stayed in farm homes whenever she could, and often travelled by train. She would accept no more than one dollar from any donor. She knew well enough that her future constituents were not rich.

Wherever she spoke, the halls were packed. She talked about the great drop in farm prices, she talked about education, and she pointed out what she saw as the many errors of the Conservative government.

"The protective tariff," she told her audiences, "makes everything you need to buy, whether it's shoes for the children or implements for the farm, too dear. Your produce and dairy products are being sold too cheap."

Her listeners shouted, "Hear, hear!" She was telling them what they already knew, but she was saying it out loud and in public.

"The protective tariff is a way," she went on, "to put money into the pockets of the already rich and to make the poor poorer. It is the wealthy who are keeping farm prices down."

Standing on the back of a wagon in a barn, surrounded by hay bales and the smell of horses, she talked to the farmers about her opponent, the sitting member for South-East Grey. "What has your Conservative member of Parliament done for you? In all his time in the House of Commons, Mr. Ball has scarcely opened his mouth."

She had a deep, pleasing voice, and all that she had learned from listening to her father's friends, from her own experience, and from the people she had met on her way, combined to give her confidence. The men and women who heard her speak soon understood that Miss Macphail would not be a silent representative if they elected her to the House of Commons.

While she was making her speeches in the local towns and villages, the Protestant ministers in the area decided to preach sermons on different religions. Just before the election, knowing Agnes's affiliation, some of them attacked the Church of the Latter-day Saints. They spoke darkly of polygamy, although the Latter-day Saints had long since abandoned the practice. They hinted at other and worse goings-on. These "sermons" were an underhand way for some clergymen to let their congregations know that they disapproved of Agnes Macphail. They were running a little anyone-but-Agnes campaign of their own. Or were they telling the voters to elect anyone-but-a-woman?

Not all the women Agnes spoke to were on her side, either. "She should leave all this to the men," they said. "What can she do? They'll take no notice of a female in Ottawa."

By the time election day came round, Agnes was exhausted. She had travelled hundreds of miles by rail. Sometimes kind farmers had lent her their cars and she had been able then to drive to the separate ridings. For weeks at a time, she had slept in a different bed each night. She had talked, had debated, had answered hundreds of questions.

But were the voters of South-East Grey ready to send a woman to Ottawa? That was the big question. Even a woman who knew their problems inside out? Even a woman who was devoted to their cause?

"Am I to become a member of Parliament," she asked herself, "or to remain a teacher with an outside interest in politics?" And there were times in those last hours before the election when she thought fondly of her life in the classroom, her days of being greeted every morning by rows of cheerful faces.

"If there's a heavy snowfall," she said to her sisters, "the farmers won't be able to get out to vote and then I'm done for."

But December 6, 1921 was a clear day. Voters turned out in their horse-and-buggies and their motorcars in good numbers. It was a long day, a day of suspense, not just for Agnes but for her family and all those who had helped her.

Dougald and Etta Macphail looked on with mixed feelings. They could see nothing but difficulties ahead for a woman in the political arena. Their daughter had so far met with admiration and success in her life. She had a good career. Was she reaching out too far? And if she failed, what then?

Throughout the day, friends and neighbours gathered in the Ceylon farmhouse and drank tea and coffee and waited. And waited. By evening, nerves were frayed. One neighbour had his ear to the phone and was calling out the returns as they came in. One by one, the farming areas fell to Agnes. At every success, the crowd in the house cheered.

And then Donald Stewart put the phone down and said solemnly, "Friends, we have made history in the constituency of South-East Grey. We have elected the first woman to the Parliament of Canada."

The cheers and applause in that farmhouse kitchen nearly raised the roof.

Agnes Macphail was thirty-one years old and she had achieved an almost impossible goal. She was a woman from a rural area, a country schoolteacher. She had overcome family opposition, illness, and other setbacks and she had won a seat in the House of Commons in Ottawa.

It was her moment of triumph. Not only had she won, with 2,598 votes more than Mr. Ball, but she had the largest majority ever gained in the constituency.

There was great rejoicing that night as Agnes and all her supporters and party workers went to nearby Durham to celebrate.

"Without," she insisted later, "the benefit of alcohol."

Modest in victory, she said, "Any candidate who had been the choice of the United Farmers in that campaign would have won."

The newspapers had other views: "If oratory consists in being able to attract and hold the intense interest of an audience…in being able to convince them that her ideas are sound, then Miss Macphail is one of the finest orators in the Dominion of Canada today," said the *Woodstock Sentinel Review*.

"The lady wears skirts, but they do not appear to be much of an impediment when she takes a notion to run," said the *Flesherton Advance*.

The *Toronto Star* called Agnes, "the aggressive lady who enlivened the proceedings of the Tariff Commission last December."

She had won by the largest majority of any Progressive Party candidate in the province.

In January of 1922, the newly elected member for South-East Grey went to Ottawa to look at the Parliament Buildings, the place where she hoped to make her pitch for the farming community. She gazed at the imposing stone walls, the green copper roof, the turrets, the Victoria Tower as it was then called, and she was overwhelmed.

"They were all I had imagined and more," she said of that moment. "My devotion to Canada was so great, and my nerves so taut, that tears sprang to my eyes."

The sergeant-at-arms remembered Miss Agnes Macphail's visit on that cold day. "I was very favourably impressed by her evident sincerity of manner and the frank fearlessness of her conversation," he said.

To her eyes, though, the inside of the building was over-luxurious; the offices were large; the carpets, the hangings, and wood panelling were very different from the simpler places she knew and a far cry indeed from the log house of her childhood.

When she was offered a bigger office than those given to others, she refused it. She wanted to make it clear from the start that she needed no special treatment just because she was a woman.

"All I want," she said, "is equality, the same respect that is accorded to the men." It didn't seem a great deal to ask, but she soon found it was more than her colleagues were prepared to give.

She returned home to Ceylon after that January visit more determined than ever to work hard for her constituents.

In the previous session of Parliament, the representatives of the farmers' unions in the House had decided to call themselves the National Progressive Party. The new party, led by the Honorable T.A. Crerar, was recognized as the third party in Parliament.

The leader of the Conservative Party, Arthur Meighen, attacked the Progressives at once. "The farmers' political movement," he said, "promotes not only Free Trade but contains socialistic, bolshevistic and Soviet nonsense."

William Lyon Mackenzie King, leader of the Liberals and prime minister, welcomed the Progressives into the House of Commons as a wolf welcomes sheep into his lair. He saw them as people who were meant to be Liberals and whom he would lure over to his side.

The new party with sixty-five elected members had enough seats to become the official Opposition. Feeling that they lacked political experience and undecided amongst themselves – many of them believed that they should vote each one according to conscience – they chose not to accept this role. The fifty elected Conservatives became the party in opposition instead.

∞

In March 1922, a medium-sized woman wearing glasses, wearing a plain blue serge dress that had cost her forty-five dollars and, at that price, was meant to last, arrived in the capital city to take her place among the men in the House of Commons.

"How could I have known that my clothes, my eating habits, the way I talked, would be remarked on in every detail by the reporters who attended the sessions. I had thought they would take notice of my ideas."

The women of the press, who might have been expected to support her, attacked her clothes, her lack of style, and her forthright behaviour. They exaggerated her words and picked on her mannerisms. She was a woman and she was, it appeared, fair game.

During interviews, Agnes wanted to talk politics, but reporters were more interested in the fact that she didn't wear a hat in the House of Commons.

Male reporters, too, found her an easy target: She looked "bleak and severe."

"Does Agnes know what love is?"

"Do you think it possible to go into political life and yet keep radiant and untarnished the inner shrine of a woman's modesty, delicacy, and sensitiveness?"

What a question!

She had, as always, an answer. "I surely do," she responded. "Public life broadens, not blunts, a woman's makeup."

She had no time for the kind of social chitchat expected by some reporters, and her short answers did little to help her image. As she learned to be wary, she was thought hard and difficult. She had gone to Ottawa with ideals and with the hope of working in a co-operative way for the country's good. The wall of opposition she hit in those first months made her very unhappy and marked the rest of her years in the House.

One man said that now she had shown that a woman could be elected, she had proved her point and would soon return "with relief...to the obscurity of a little school in the back concessions."

He didn't know Agnes Macphail.

∞

What was Agnes Macphail from Proton Township thinking of on the March day when she walked in procession behind the Gentleman Usher of the Black Rod to the Red Chamber, to be received by the Queen's representative? Surrounded by men, she imagined all the women who would follow after her. "I could almost hear them coming," she said. But it was to be a long time before those female footsteps were more than a sound in her head.

In the Red Chamber, the Governor General, Lord Byng, an imposing figure in a red robe and long white wig, instructed the members of the House in their duties in the session about to begin. Listening to him, unaware of the unpleasant treatment she was about to receive, Agnes felt proud and happy. She had made it. She was here to make a difference and she was determined to do so.

∽

"When I came into the House of Commons and walked out into the lobby, men sprang to their feet. I asked them to sit down since I'd come to walk around. I didn't want them to do me any favours. I figured I was going to have trouble enough. I was right. I found I couldn't quietly do my job without being ballyhooed like the bearded lady...I was a curiosity, a freak. And you know how they treat freaks."

At first the men were courteous. They made fine speeches of welcome to her. They hoped, the other members said, "... that she will find political life pleasant and will exercise a refining influence on our assembly."

She was delighted, too, to find red roses on her desk that first day. Members of Mackenzie King's cabinet came to greet her. She glowed. She was used to admiration from students, teachers, those who heard her speak, and she felt that she was about to go on being treated in that way. But she very quickly found that there was to be no bed of roses in this arena. Had her parents been right when they feared for her survival in this men's club?

Among her new colleagues were men who bitterly opposed everything she stood for. And before long, the kind words gave way to jibes. Even the roses, she discovered, were a joke, the result of a bet. It became obvious that a number of these men resented her presence. A woman in their world! How dare she! To many of them, she could never be an equal, she would always be "only a woman."

∞

One of her first moves did nothing to make her popular. "When people are living on very little," she said, "a Member of Parliament's salary at four thousand dollars is much too high. Twenty-five hundred dollars is enough for anybody to live on."

She promptly returned fifteen hundred dollars to the treasury.

She was attacked by MPs with families who often had to keep up two homes, and she soon discovered that the expenses of being a politician and living in the capital were much greater than she had bargained for. Later on she accepted the full amount, but for the moment she was seen as a woman who had no idea of what it cost to raise a family, and as a troublemaker.

Who were they, the members of the Progressive party among whom Agnes now spent her days? Robert Gardiner from Medicine Hat represented the United Farmers of Alberta. He had won a by-election with a huge majority. George Coote, Henry Spencer, and Ted Garland had come from quiet country backgrounds. Many of the new members had grown up on farms. They were passionate about what they stood for, but like Agnes, they were not used to the ways of politics in the capital.

T.A. Crerar resigned as House leader of the party that same year. He needed more time for other work, he said. But he also had different views from some of the Alberta and Ontario members. Robert Forke succeeded him as leader.

Agnes's friends knew her as a warm and caring person, but she soon had the reputation in Ottawa of being a "warped spinster." It was a common label for unmarried women in those times. Because she had no husband and no children, she was deprived of "love" and must therefore be bitter and difficult.

Agnes felt this misjudgment deeply. Every insult, every wounding comment, gave her pain. She was fortunate in having a kind landlady, Mrs. Quay. At home in the evenings, she could relax and pour out her woes. Mrs. Quay gave her sympathy and comfort and, later on, advice on what to wear when she was invited to grand events at Rideau Hall.

In the House, the lone woman was lonely. If she ate in the House of Commons dining room, she was stared at "as if I might eat peas off my knife." She found it easier to eat alone in a downtown restaurant. She began to lose weight.

But she knew that if she failed, if she let the men win, she would be betraying not only all the people who had elected her but also those women of the future who were to follow in her footsteps to the Red Chamber.

In the midst of all this work, these speeches, the occasional grand dinner parties, this was a miserable time for Agnes. She had blazed a trail for women, and yet women reporters were writing stories about her that were unkind and often inaccurate. She knew she had the experience, the knowledge, to make a difference. And yet most of her colleagues continued to be hostile to her. When she came into a committee room, they would make a point of rising to their feet and putting their pipes and cigarettes away just as they would have done in any drawing room. But this was not a drawing room and Agnes was not a society lady. From the public gallery of the House, visitors would stare down at her as if she were a strange animal in the zoo.

She had made hundreds of speeches elsewhere boldly and bravely, but in the House she was nervous and fearful. She said at the time to a group of electors, "If you are picking a candidate, pick a strong one who is able to go up against that wall of steel."

∞

The session at last came to an end and Agnes was able to go home. Once more, just as she had done after her first year of teaching, she spent some of her salary on a generous gift for her parents. A few days after she got home, the present was delivered, and she asked them to come outside to see what she had bought for them.

What they saw was a shiny new sleigh. Agnes had even bought a lap robe to keep them warm as they drove around the winter roads. She looked at them, waiting for smiles of delight.

"How could you spend your money like this?" her mother cried.

"We'll be getting rid of the horses when we move," Dougald added.

There was an argument. Agnes went off to visit friends. Her father went out to the shed to hide his anger. They made up, but it was a hurt that stayed with Agnes for a long time.

When they were speaking again, Dougald, knowing of the difficult time she'd had, asked Agnes if she really wanted to go back to the House of Commons. No one would blame her if she chose to return to teaching. She had done well in Ottawa, shown what a woman could achieve. She could quit with honour.

It was a temptation, and Agnes thought for a moment or two of the young folk she might influence and teach in the coming years. But she knew it would be a retreat from the battlefield. And was she not Agnes Campbell Macphail with Scottish blood in her veins! She would return to the House of Commons and she would return fighting.

Agnes Macphail, MP

The Co-operative Commonwealth Federation, the new party
that dreamed of changing the lives of the working classes.

4

Dreaming of a New Society

Inside a cottage in Glace Bay, Nova Scotia, a baby almost too weak to cry lay in a broken-down crib. A child with scrawny arms, dressed in a ragged shirt, chewed on a crust. Their mother pointed hopelessly to an empty cupboard. The man of the house, his skin grimy from long hours working in the coal mine, stood by, silent and angry. Agnes Macphail, walking away in despair, knowing that there were dozens of scenes like this in the town, could only promise to speak out on behalf of the miners when she returned to Ottawa.

When Agnes was born, there were about five million people living in this huge country and most of them lived in the rural areas. In her lifetime, the population grew to fifteen million. The liners that took the rich to Europe for their world tours brought back another cargo – immigrants from Russia, from the British Isles, and from all parts of Europe. They were coming from overcrowded places to a land where fortunes were made. They had heard of the gold rush in the Yukon and of the great farmland on the Prairies and of the opportunities in the growing cities.

More children meant that more schools were needed. In 1917, the Winnipeg *Eaton's Catalogue* advertised school building kits for sale. And before long these prefabricated one-room schoolhouses dotted the Prairies.

People were moving from the farms to make money in the fast-growing cities. Factories sprouted like mushrooms to produce more goods, and this meant more jobs.

It could have been wonderful. But some of the men who were making money from industry were greedy. The longer hours they could get the men and women in the factories to work, the more goods were made and the more profit there was for the owners of the factories and mines.

Two years before she was elected, Agnes had read about the Winnipeg General Strike. Thirty thousand men and women left their jobs to protest against their working conditions and to seek better wages. The workers also wanted to form stronger unions. The police and firemen and postal workers all joined the strike and the city was shut down. The employers and bankers and politicians joined together to attack the workers. As usual, "Bolshevik agitators" were blamed for the strike, and when the strike continued, the Mounties were called in to beat back the strikers. Mike Sokolowski, a registered alien, was shot through the heart and killed, and many were injured. Some of the leaders were put in jail. The workers were never given a chance to put their case forward, and relations between employers and employees were even worse than before.

The *Manitoba Free Press* headline read, "This is Class War!"

The Russian revolution had happened only five years earlier. At first many in the western world had seen the revolution as the courageous rising of a brave people against tyranny. Very soon, it appeared that in the ongoing bloody struggle, one ruthless regime had been replaced by another and this one run by the workers. Anti-union politicians were able to point to events in Russia as an example of what could happen if the workers were allowed to band together. It was a weapon they would use for many years.

Agnes was prepared to be called any names – "Bolshevik," "red menace" – in her struggle for equality. In her speech on the situation in Glace Bay she said: "The British Empire Steel Corporation is threatening to cut the miners' wages. The government gives this company subsidies and yet the miners and their families do not have enough to live on. What do you propose to do about it?"

The prime minister answered patronizingly that the measures the government took to improve matters were always a step in the right direction.

"Ah yes," Agnes responded. "Very mincing steps."

A group of women from a benevolent society had been to Glace Bay to see the conditions and had come back reporting that all was well. The stories of starvation and hardship were exaggerated, they said. It was clear to Agnes that these ladies had been shown a "Potemkin" village, a few homes and families made to appear comfortable just for their visit.

Some politicians blamed "communist lies" for all the sad stories they were hearing from Nova Scotia.

But Agnes had seen the poverty and exhaustion and empty cupboards for herself. She took note of the pernicious system by which the Company kept the miners in a kind of serfdom. The miners had to buy goods from the company store. Once they got into debt, the money was deducted from their wages, and if they owed more than was due to them, they were often fired. As there was no welfare system, no unemployment insurance, the people were without hope and left with no option but to beg.

"I think the labour men, the miners, should be given every opportunity to organize, and that the almost contemptuous propaganda that has been circulated against class organization in this country should cease," Agnes said.

In response to shouts of "Communist" and "Bolshevik lies," she said, "No one there looked 'red' to me, and if I lived there, I would be a lot 'redder' than anything I saw."

All the government subsidies, bonuses, and tariff protection given to the British Empire Steel Company were "… an example of the pampering of industry and the neglect of humanity."

Her strong words and those of her colleagues stirred the government to action. The Glace Bay miners' lives improved slowly, and whenever she went there, Agnes was welcomed in Nova Scotia as a saviour. "Our own people do not forget," they told her. And for years, a ballad was sung in the area: "God give us more women like Agnes Macphail. When the miners were hungry she never did fail."

The farmers' representatives were now the largest single group in the House. They had come to Parliament to defend their rights against the interests of the industrial powers. They were not looking for revolution. The very word "revolution" at that time was enough to drive people to the far right. But the struggle was and remained, in a way, "a class war." The harder the Progressives fought for a better deal, the louder the Conservative members shouted, "Communist conspiracy."

∽

When a member spoke of "common labourers," Agnes replied indignantly, "We do not sufficiently respect those who toil with their hands."

Her grandparents, her parents, her whole family all knew what it was to spend their days from dawn until dusk tilling the soil, caring for the animals, simply making the wheels of ordinary life turn around.

The Liberals at this time needed all the votes they could get and were poaching members of the Progressive Party. Mackenzie King twice offered Agnes a seat in his cabinet if she would change sides. Agnes declined. But King managed to lure away T.A. Crerar, the Progressives' first leader, and, to Agnes's dismay, his successor, Robert Forke.

There were divisions among the remaining Progressives. Some of them, like Agnes, had come to see that the only way for the farmers to get a fair deal was to start a co-operative movement, a sharing of market opportunities. This handful of like-minded people became known as the Ginger Group. They were not about to form another party on the lines of the two old ones. It was time to change.

Agnes boldly stated the new group's view. "There are two kinds of government – the one in which the parties aspire to Power and thus perpetuate competitiveness in matters of legislation. This system as we have seen it has brought the world near to ruin. The other is the democratically organized group which aims for co-operation to secure justice rather than to compete for power."

The Ginger Group held its own meetings but joined with J.S. Woodsworth and others to promote the best interests of farmers and industrial workers.

And then came something that all the politicians in the world couldn't have foreseen: The Great Depression. The soil on the prairies turned to dust. On the financial markets, fortunes were lost overnight. Men and women who had led comfortable lives were now begging on the streets, or riding the rails to find jobs elsewhere. There was such a shortage of gas that cars were being drawn along by horses.

There had been a change of government, and the Conservative prime minister, R.B. Bennett, kept on saying that all was well, and if it wasn't, things would improve before long. He didn't see the backstreets of the cities, where people with their feet wrapped in newspaper against the winter cold rummaged in garbage cans for food.

Agnes knew of them. She stood up in the House and said, "We picture the prime minister in his absolute, assured, and complete comfort this winter, holding out to the unemployed the one hope that if they emerge from the present crisis, they will be better people, strengthened by the fire of adversity."

Many did not "emerge." With no relief for the unemployed and no medical help, children died of disease and many adults never recovered from these years when they were weakened by a lack of decent food.

Hundreds of raggedly dressed, pale, malnourished people, all unemployed, gathered on Parliament Hill in a quiet protest. It was a sad crowd – some of them barely had the strength to stand up, let alone shout. But R.B. Bennett sent out the RCMP to control them and beat them back.

Agnes was furious. "They were unarmed, destitute folk. Did the government need this show of force?"

∞

The time had come to create a new, more forceful party, one that would embrace all the workers, not only the farmers. Agnes had been to Europe and had seen in Scandinavia that social democracy could work for the people. The schools there encouraged a spirit of community service in the pupils. There was medical care for all and the poor were not abandoned by the state. She wanted the same benefits for the Canadian people, every single one of them.

It was an exciting day in Toronto when the new party, the Co-operative Commonwealth Federation (CCF), held its first general meeting. Bold words were spoken from the platform.

"We aim to replace the present capitalist system, to build a new social order in which individuality will not be crushed out by regimentation."

"We will establish in Canada a Co-operative Commonwealth in which the principle regulating production, distribution, and exchange will be the supplying of human needs and not the making of profits."

It was the largest meeting of men and women from labour and agriculture in Canadian history. Many were turned away, and the organizers had to hire a second hall.

Agnes was full of excitement. As she stood there on the platform with her colleagues, James Shaver Woodsworth, the leader of the new party, and Robert Gardiner from Alberta, and looked out over the eager faces in that crowded hall, Agnes could see her dream of a better society coming true. She looked out over the faces in this crowded hall and knew that things could change. The CCF would make it happen. And she shouted out the slogan for the new movement, "Come Comrades, Forward."

"I claim," said Woodsworth, "that we have come to a period in our history when we must decide, once and for all, which shall prevail, profits or human welfare."

J.S. Woodsworth was a remarkable man, and Agnes always felt herself fortunate to stand beside him in their struggle to help the working people. He became known as "the Conscience of the House of Commons," and he was respected by members of all parties. He had started his professional life as a Methodist Minister but felt he could help people better by working among them than by preaching to them. He had worked as a lumberjack and a teacher and often had to spend time away from his large family to do what he felt was right.

He saw the new party as one that would bring benefits to all kinds of workers, not only the farmers. And one thing he wanted to make clear: "The CCF," he said, "will have nothing to do with Communism."

But many people were afraid of these new ideas, especially businessmen and factory owners. R.B. Bennett said, "... this propaganda is being put forward by organizations from foreign lands," once again dragging out the red bogeyman.

The leader of the Communist party in Canada, Tim Buck, was sent to jail. Agnes herself was barred from speaking in certain halls and clubs because she was seen as "left-wing" and therefore a threat to security – the security of the well-to-do.

But all the opposition only made the MP for South-East Grey even more determined to speak out whenever she could on behalf of the ordinary working man and woman.

Glenbow Archives

Glenbow Archives

Robert Gardiner, MP. A faithful friend who loved her.
She couldn't give up her work to marry him, or any man.

5

Lone Woman in a Male Arena

Agnes was standing on the platform in the village hall talking about the advantages of the co-operative system when a heckler called out, "Why don't you get a husband!" Agnes asked the man to stand up. He did so, smiling, pleased with himself.

"Are you married?" Agnes asked him.

"Yes I am," he replied.

Agnes turned to the audience and said, "I bet he wasn't like this when his wife married him ten years ago." Then she looked the heckler up and down over her spectacles and asked, "What guarantee do I have that in ten years' time any man I married wouldn't turn out to be like you?"

The audience burst out laughing, and as the unhappy man sat down Agnes was able to continue.

Agnes didn't despise men. Several men made her offers of marriage at this time of her life. A friend once said that every elderly man she met in that part of Ontario boasted that he had once proposed to Agnes Macphail. But Agnes was not to be caught.

"When I hear men talk about women being the angels of the home, I always, mentally at least, shrug my shoulders in doubt. I do not want to be the angel of any home; I want for myself what I want for other women, absolute equality. After that is secured, then men and women can take turns at being angels."

She made that speech during a debate on the Divorce Bill. It was one of her most famous and most often quoted statements.

She never joined a women's suffrage group or spoke of feminism. She was not an activist. She was simply active. When women came to her with their problems, she did what she could to help them. All her life, she worked to make things better for women in the workplace, for women in prison, for equality everywhere. Besides all that, she was an example to women; where she had gone, they could follow. She was an inspiration, and she wasn't the only woman out there, blazing a trail.

She gave a speech at a meeting of the Canadian Alliance for Women's Vote in Quebec entitled, "Whither Woman?" Women in Quebec could vote in federal elections, but it was 1940 before they were granted the right to vote in their own provincial elections. And the woman who worked very hard to bring this about was Thérèse Casgrain.

Mme Casgrain joined the Co-operative Commonwealth Federation and started the Quebec Branch of the Voice of Women. She wrote a book called *A Woman In A Man's World*, which showed the kind of difficulties Agnes had endured. Like Agnes, she never gave up the fight, and eventually she became a senator.

The Senate kept its doors closed to women long after they had been allowed to enter the House of Commons. The men in charge were interpreting the words of the British North America Act to suit themselves. Instead of referring to "men and women" in many of its clauses, the BNA Act used the word "persons." And "persons" had been adjudged to refer only to men.

Judge Emily Murphy with four other women set out to challenge this.

"Are women not 'persons' too?" Judge Murphy asked.

The nine men on the Supreme Court of Canada answered resoundingly, "No!"

"If women are not 'persons' what are they?" Agnes demanded of the men in the House.

Judge Murphy and her friends didn't let the matter rest. They took their case to the Judicial Commitee of the Privy Council in London, England.

That imposing group stated that the idea of keeping women from public office was "a relic of days more barbarous than ours." So the red-robed stuffed shirts on the Canadian Supreme Court had to give way and allow that women were "persons" after all.

Agnes rejoiced with the others at this victory, although she herself had no ambition to move to the upper chamber.

Referring to the Senate, she once said, "I would hate to see a woman wasted there. It is a useless institution and appointment to it would be like being placed on a shelf prior to burial."

All the same, she was not prepared to see any of her sex barred from any public office: it was a matter of equality and a matter of choice.

Agnes had many other allies in this particular fight. In 1921, the same year that Agnes Macphail took her seat in the House of Commons, Nellie McClung was elected to the Alberta Legislature. McClung was known as a novelist as well as a tireless promoter of women's issues. One of her books, *Sowing Seeds in Danny*, became a bestseller. Older than Agnes, she wrote long letters of advice to her, encouraging her to keep on with the difficult struggle.

Charlotte Whitton, who later became mayor of Ottawa, was another fighter for women's rights. She and Agnes differed on one important point. When Whitton referred to women playing an equal role in politics, she meant single women. Married women should stay at home, she felt. Agnes, while not prepared to get married herself, saw no reason why a married woman should not have a career as well as a family.

∞

What was Agnes Macphail like at this time in her life, in her mid-thirties? It depended on whom you asked. Her women friends saw her as attractive, a tall, slim woman, almost romantic-looking in the capes she liked to wear. Some saw her as angular, severe, plain. To her family she was generous and kind. Her young nieces knew her as an aunt who loved to go shopping with them and who never forgot a birthday.

She began to take more care with her clothes, choosing the right colours, wearing a little jewellery. But when she came into a room, it wasn't her black dress and gold bracelet that made people stop and notice her, it was her personality.

Some men only saw in her a harsh demanding "spinster."

One male journalist described her as "not exactly lovable."

She saw herself as a plain woman, not cut out for romance.

They were all wrong.

She had earned much respect from the men in her party. Among these few Agnes found the friendship and pleasure that had been so much missing from her first year or two in Parliament. She also found love. Or rather love found her.

The first member of the Ginger Group to offer her his hand was Preston Elliot of Ontario. It was a sincere proposal from a man who truly admired her. This was a man whose ideals were the same as hers, a man she liked. She could picture the house, evenings by the fire spent talking of the events of the day, a couple of children, a place where Santa Claus did know the address. But the picture faded as she considered the reality.

She thanked Mr. Elliot kindly for his offer but said, "I cannot now desert the constituents of South-East Grey." The truth was that she could not face the idea of becoming a politician's wife instead of a being a politician in her own right.

Another man who proposed to her was so upset when she refused him that he said, "When I do marry, don't phone and don't wire; I want to forget I ever knew you."

The next one to come courting was Robert Gardiner from Alberta. He was a serious man, a dear friend, devoted to Agnes. They shared the same views and both were dedicated to their work. She respected and admired him. But the same question in her mind had to be answered. Her career or his? His home or hers? When she said "no" to him, he felt the rejection deeply. He withdrew from federal politics and returned to Alberta. When he died, he left his small estate to Agnes Macphail.

Turning down Robert Gardiner wasn't an easy or quick decision for Agnes to make. She knew that the road ahead could be lonely for a woman, especially in those times. She would have liked a partner and a real home but wanted to devote herself to the work that she had chosen and that she felt had chosen her.

She continued to pound away at the barriers that kept women from certain jobs. It was, as she saw it, the ingrained attitude not just of men but of both sexes that kept women in their place. She had plenty to say about that "place."

One problem that was holding women back, she said, was "the cult of the lady." The "lady" was that woman who embroidered pillowslips and handker-chiefs, poured tea, and was, as the song said, "so nice to come home to."

"Be independent!" was her message to women. "Woman's place WAS once in the home. The daughter was apprenticed to the mother and learned her skills. We must turn to ourselves for wisdom and not falter. Women have been smothered by centuries of not questioning what John said."

When she spoke, she recalled how her own life had very nearly been just such an apprenticeship leading to a "place" very different from the one in which she now spent her days. She never entered the House of Commons, in spite of the mean treatment she had received, without a sense of awe. The wide lobby, the pillars, the beautiful wood panelling, the fact that John A. Macdonald and other famous men had walked here, all gave her a deep feeling of pride. And over time, she knew it was where she belonged.

∞

When she nervously stood up in the House to make her very first speech it was in a debate about a change to the Elections Act.

Foreign-born women who had moved to Canada were to be allowed a vote IF they were married to Canadian men. Agnes felt that foreign-born women should be allowed to vote in Canada whether they married Canadian men or not.

"I think," she said, "that women just want to be individuals. No more and no less."

She often wished aloud that there were more women in Parliament because, she said, "Women work for results, not the game."

∽

When she was invited to take part in a radio broadcast in 1936, an international hookup with Nancy Astor, the first woman elected to the British Parliament, and Caroline O'Day, a congresswoman from the United States, Agnes told her transatlantic listeners, "The work of the world is neither men's nor women's work but the work of both."

∽

The first session had been difficult, but she had learned much from it. When she returned to Ottawa after the break, Agnes Macphail was better prepared for the insults and the devious ways of those politicians who could pretend to agree with her while working against her behind her back. Yet there were still occasions when she would return sadly to her lodgings in the evening and wonder whether she would ever achieve even a fraction of the changes she wanted made.

As always, she was ready to jump on any statement she felt was out of place or insulting to the people she knew best.

Of one man who suggested that "servant girls" be brought into Canada from other countries, she asked, "… that 'girl' is not considered the social equal of those for whom she works. Why not?"

She leapt to the defence of the often unsung heroes of farm life: "It is true that the farmers work hard and their pay is poor. But it is also infinitely true that the farm woman's day is longer and her pay poorer."

At the end of a session, when everyone was tired and ready to head for home, Agnes brought up the matter of MPs' salaries again. She realized that the twenty-five hundred dollars she had mentioned before was too low but why not make it thirty-five hundred, let all the members return five hundred dollars to the government.

The argument for raising salaries to four thousand dollars in the first place had been that it would do away with the party fund and make the members free of party ties, free to vote as they thought best. This had not happened.

"The best proof that this is not so is the voting as we have witnessed it in this House," Agnes said.

Shouts of, "Withdraw!" echoed round the chamber.

"How much did the honourable member receive herself?"

"The honourable member doth protest too much," she called out in response.

"Withdraw," they kept on shouting at her, and as she looked around, all she could see were hostile faces.

The leader of her own party, Robert Forke, leaned over and told her softly to withdraw. She apologized and said, "I have no desire to reflect on the honour of any member of this House."

More cries of "Withdraw!"

Agnes, uncowed, went on to say, "I will withdraw the statement if it is unparliamentary and beg everybody's pardon. The thing I want to say, if I may be allowed to do so, is this: When some of the good party men have declared their views outside the House on certain matters and we see them come in and vote in the opposite way, what are we to think?"

∽

Her early years in Ottawa weren't all taken up with work. She never lost her love of dancing and she liked a good party. But she never got into the habit of accepting invitations simply for political reasons. She wasn't the woman to seek the favour or approval of the high and the mighty.

She had learned early on to be self-reliant, and being among the men in Parliament only made her more so. She ended a speech to a group of young women, "Do not rely completely on any one human being, however dear. We meet all life's greatest tests alone."

If she had been hurt and set back by the treatment she received at first, she had also become a fearful opponent. A member from Quebec got up to say that the farmers in his riding had a good life in their log cabins and foolishly went on to say, "They are satisfied with very little – indeed sometimes nothing at all."

Agnes jumped up and asked, "Does the honourable member live as his constituents do...?"

Laughter drowned out the unfortunate man's response.

Probably very few members of the House knew as much as she did about that "very little" and "nothing at all" and the effect it had on the women who were trying to keep those log-cabin homes going.

Agnes Macphail's voice in that male arena was a lone voice, but it was becoming a very powerful voice indeed.

Agnes Macphail, MP.
In the worst of times she stood her ground and kept on fighting.

6

Agnes on Trial

W hen she was eighteen, Agnes was walking to the Normal School in Stratford to take the entrance examination when she found herself beside the grim walls of the jail. As she walked, she had been happily imagining herself in front of her first class of students and recalling how only three years ago her own future had loomed ahead like a prison sentence. Then she looked up and saw a square of black cloth hanging from the flagpole. The horror of it sent a chill right through her. Everyone knew that when the black flag was hoisted a prisoner was to be hanged that day. She pictured the man in his cell waiting to by killed by order of the law and wondered if anyone ever deserved to be put to death that way.

☙

Years later a smartly dressed woman marched up to the gates of Kingston Penitentiary and demanded to be let in. She was a member of Parliament and therefore had the right to visit any public institution. So many stories had come to her about the dreadful treatment of prisoners, it was as if a thousand voices were calling out for her help. So Agnes Macphail had come to see for herself. And what she saw was enough to make her ill.

Sick convicts were lying in the corridors; men with tuberculosis were not kept apart from the rest of the prisoners, and infection spread. Cries from mentally ill men echoed round the cells. Inmates were beaten severely with leather straps, often for trivial offences. They were held in shackles for long periods with their hands above their heads and kept in solitary confinement for weeks at a time. The cells were filthy, the food appalling. No effort was made to reform the men and women in prisons.

When she got back to the House and looked around at all those comfortable and free men, Agnes demanded that something be done.

"Are our prisons intended to be nothing more than whipping institutions and places of vengeance?" she asked.

In one place the bathwater was being used to wash dishes, and mice ran in and out of the flour bins in the kitchens. Teenage boys were put in the same cells as hardened criminals. Women were often sexually abused by the guards.

Telling of her visit to the women's section of Kingston Penitentiary, she said, "As I faced those women, I did not feel different from them; I simply felt that I had been in much more fortunate circumstances."

This attitude alone made her seem strange to those who could see only that the people in jail were criminals and deserved all the harsh treatment they got.

∞

The men and women running the prisons were often ill-qualified. Most of them appeared to be untrained and uncaring. They were simply keepers of the key. And their superiors were complacent. The jobs in the system were often gifts of members of Parliament, who could fill the posts with their friends and relatives.

"These men are usually," she said, "the brother, cousin, or brother-in-law of someone in authority."

This did not make her popular with the MPs whose brothers and cousins and brothers-in-law had jobs as wardens and guards.

But her main concern was with the prisoners themselves. At this time, nearly three-quarters of released convicts returned to jail for other offences, many of them more than once.

In 1925, Agnes Macphail introduced a resolution in the House to provide work for the prison inmates. Any proceeds would go to their dependants or be saved till their release. The labour unions raised no objections to the proposal, and others supported it. Only much later was this system put in place.

When she and her colleagues persisted in their attempts to show the appalling flaws in the prison system, they were accused of being communist agitators. Any inmate who tried to fight for better conditions was also labelled a communist. There were people who wanted very much to stop these "do-gooders" and "reformers" and would go to any lengths to achieve their aim.

Agnes, always ready to listen to the unfortunates who had spent time in prison, was about to give her enemies the chance they'd been waiting for.

One evening in 1929, when she was working late and her secretary had gone home, a well-dressed, well-spoken man made his way into her office.

"I know you work on behalf of prisoners," he said. "I myself have been in jail. But I have turned my life around. I try now to help those in trouble. My name is Charles Baynes."

Agnes accepted all that Charles Baynes told her: He received a war veteran's pension because of tuberculosis brought on during his war service. He was now helping other veterans to get their full pensions. Because of his contacts, he could help Agnes in her work.

Some members of the press were on her side too. Harry Anderson, a reporter for the *Globe*, wrote, "It seems impossible to look for straightforward and truthful statements from the Minister of Justice or its officialdom on any matter affecting the penitentiary." And a headline in the same newspaper condensed the situation into one sentence: "Motive at Kingston is to break hearts not to reform men." Anderson became one of Agnes's strongest supporters.

A woman like Agnes Macphail was bound to make enemies, and in the Honourable Hugh Guthrie she had a formidable foe. She was outspoken, she hung on to her causes like a dog to a bone, and she had crossed Guthrie before. When he had tried to tell the farmers that higher tariffs were good for them, Agnes had denounced him. She knew, and made it clear, that higher tariffs were damaging to the farmers.

When Guthrie became minister of justice in R.B. Bennett's Conservative government, he resented this woman speaking out as she did for prison reform. It reflected badly on his department and on him. He wanted people to understand that he was making changes, if slowly. He said his department was well run and that these people were making a fuss about nothing.

The government alleged that the riots in Kingston jail had been caused by "communists." An ex-inmate named Price who had been shot by guards while in prison contradicted this. The riots would have happened anyway, he said, because prisoners were "fed up" with their treatment. And, he warned, the next riots would be worse.

Few people were inclined to listen to a jailbird, but everything he said struck a chord with Agnes and the other reformers. The boys of fifteen and sixteen who were put in cells with hardened criminals, Price said, would cry at first, but before long, they were asking where they could get a "gat," the slang expression for a handgun.

In 1932, Agnes asked again for a royal commission to be set up to enquire into the prison system. Nothing had changed. There was still very little medical help given to prisoners who were ill. One man who had been shot by a guard while he was in his cell received no treatment for two days. In another jail, a sick prisoner lying in the corridor died while the commission members were visiting the prison.

All the stories Agnes heard and what she saw in her prison visits made her ready to believe anything. She was angry that after all the statements, the pleadings, the stories told in the House and in the press, nothing was being done.

And then, in 1933, Baynes contacted Agnes and told her that the Pensions Branch was out to get him and that he would soon be thrown in jail again.

"If I have to go back to that hell-hole, I will surely die," he said.

He begged Agnes to have him sent to a farm prison where he might have an easier life and fresh air.

Agnes went to Hugh Guthrie and asked him for help in the matter. "Baynes is an ex-serviceman with a good record," she said on his behalf, "surely this can be arranged."

Guthrie responded with pleasant words. He would see what he could do.

At last, on February 14, 1934, Agnes Macphail got her long-awaited chance to speak in the House on prison reform. It was in more ways than one to be her "day in court." As always, she spoke well. She told of all the injustices that she had found in the system. She even thanked the minister of justice for giving her this chance to make her case. And then she fell into Guthrie's trap. She told the story of Charles Baynes's prison experiences as he had told them to her.

Before the debate in the Commons, she had asked for Baynes's file, but it was never "available." She only discovered much later that Guthrie had given instructions that the file should be kept from her.

Guthrie was ready. He stood up, took his time, and then he read out part of Baynes's record. Baynes had been jailed several times for "indecent assault, bestiality and gross indecency."

Agnes was devastated. According to Guthrie, she had gone to bat for a man who had committed indecent acts. Homosexuality was a crime in those days, and the other charges against this man who seemed so nice, well-spoken, and helpful were appalling.

She was attacked from all sides: She was after all only a woman! She had been led astray by a good-looking man! What could you expect from a "spinster!"

No one knew that the relevant documents had been deliberately withheld from her by Guthrie. It was a terrible time and it was about to get worse. Her Conservative opponents were not going to let this chance to discredit her slip by. They spread the word in her constituency and elsewhere that she was a stupid, misguided woman. In spite of this, Agnes, being Agnes, kept on hammering away at the need for prison reform.

Guthrie didn't stop his attacks either. He went on blaming the "communists" for inventing the stories of poor conditions in jail. And then he sent an inspector, a certain Mr. Dawson, to Kingston to persuade Baynes to tell him that all of Agnes's information about prison atrocities had come from him; a "pervert" in the eyes of the world.

Through his brother, an official in the West Indies, Baynes made a plea to see Agnes again. He told her about the inspector's visit. Agnes wasn't in the mood to believe him. She knew the old saying that only a fool gets taken in by the same person twice.

Shortly after this, she was visited by an ex-convict called Hall. Inspector Dawson had visited Hall in jail and told him that Baynes was supplying Agnes Macphail with information. And then, according to Hall, the inspector said, "... when we are finished with her, she will never be able to lift up her head in the House of Commons again."

Hall was a con man, a very skilful one, but he had his own set of principles and these words offended him.

He stood there in her office and said to Agnes, "I told all this to the warden but he did nothing so I've come to tell you myself."

Agnes asked the minister of justice for the documents relating to Inspector Dawson's visit to Kingston. When she was given papers that made no reference to Baynes or Hall, she protested. Needless to say, the Honourable Hugh Guthrie told her that the papers were complete. In her absence from the House next day, he said, "Miss Macphail has asserted that one of my inspectors has talked of her to a convict while on a routine visit to the jail. This of course is not true."

Agnes was not to be put down so easily. She had the name of a prison guard who was a witness.

Guthrie then told the House that she, a poor misguided woman, had been taken in by men of low character.

At her insistence he did set up an inquiry into the matter, but it was a very narrow inquiry. Agnes had to provide and pay for her own counsel. The judge appeared to have made up his mind beforehand. Inspector Dawson denied having said anything about the honourable member for South-East Grey. He did admit having gone to Kingston to get Baynes to say he had supplied Agnes with all the bad stories about prisons.

The press had a heyday.

The St. Thomas *Times-Journal* said, "She is making a mountain out of a molehill and should forget about it."

She tried to talk to Inspector Dawson herself, but Guthrie had ordered him not to see her.

For a time it seemed as though the only witness who would speak for Agnes would be the con man, Hall. The Protestant chaplain at the prison refused to become involved in the matter.

Colonel W.B. Megloughlin, the warden of Kingston Penitentiary, did come forward. He told the inquiry that indeed Dawson had spoken to both Baynes and Hall. Dawson had told the Colonel he was afraid he had been too outspoken with Hall and that the convict might repeat what he had said. He repeated to Megloughlin the same words he had said to Hall.

"I reproached him," Megloughlin told the inquiry, "for not keeping a record of these talks with the convicts."

The Catholic chaplain, Father Kingsley, was called to the witness stand, and he, too, had talked to Dawson after his conversation with Baynes. Dawson told the chaplain that Baynes was a liar who had never had TB. Medical records stated otherwise.

Father Kingsley had worked in prisons for nearly a quarter of a century. He said that both Inspector Dawson and his chief were "full of conceit, self-opinionated, and holding the belief that experience was not necessary in prison work."

He went on, "I have seen so much inexperience, and the wreck that inexperience could make of the Kingston Penitentiary. It is very depressing and is becoming an appalling condition of affairs."

Harry Anderson, the *Globe* reporter, also appeared for Agnes and stated that he had heard one prison guard in the penitentiary say to another, "The boss wants to land Aggie."

While all this appeared to back up Agnes and her fellow reformers, the members of the commission clearly thought differently. The report they produced after their two-week hearing made no mention of Colonel Megloughlin's testimony. According to them, Hall was unreliable and Inspector Dawson had never referred to Miss Macphail. Harry Anderson's statement was ignored altogether.

As far as justice went, this was a disgrace. And it was a difficult time for Agnes Macphail. The newspapers, the gossip in Ottawa, indeed, the whole world, seemed to be against her. Her mother, who rarely showed either encouragement or sympathy, understood her distress and offered consoling words to her besieged daughter.

Meanwhile, conditions in the penitentiaries appeared to be getting worse. During his time as warden, Megloughlin had allowed the prisoners to play ball games and to talk to each other at given times. When he left, these small privileges were taken away.

But still, every chance she had, Agnes tried to bring up the matter of an independent inquiry. Hugh Guthrie kept on saying that the prison system in Canada was as good as any in the world.

Once again, the Conservatives in the House attacked Agnes, mainly for being a woman. She had given in to her "womanly sympathies" and her "sweet femininity."

And again Guthrie tried to stifle the debate. When he spoke, it was to deny any charges that were made against his department.

It wasn't until the Conservatives were voted out of office in 1935 that the Liberal minister of justice, Ernest Lapointe, finally set up the Royal Commission to Investigate the Penal System of Canada.

The chairman was to be Justice Joseph Archambault. R.W. Craig was to be another member. And to Agnes's delight, Harry Anderson, who had been on her side from the beginning, was the other.

He wrote to her, "Accept my hearty congratulations on the vindication of your courageous course... "

But the reporter died a month after he had written that letter. A little while later, Justice Archambault was taken to hospital with two broken legs. These two unrelated events made Agnes wonder if even the fates were against rectifying the horrors of Canada's penitentiaries.

At last, in October 1936, with another man appointed in Harry Anderson's place, the commission met and began to hear witnesses and to write down its findings. Agnes was called on to give her testimony, and she was able to tell what she knew to willing listeners.

The report said that special attention should be paid to:

a) the protection of society,
b) the safe custody of inmates,
c) strict but humane discipline, and
d) the *reformation* and *rehabilitation* of prisoners.

The report also recommended that a training school for prison officers should be set up on the lines of the one in Wakefield, England.

The final paragraph stated what Agnes had been trying to get across to her opponents for years. "There are very few," the commissioners wrote, "if any, prisoners who enter our penitentiaries who do not leave them worse...than when they entered."

In April 1938, Agnes received her copy of the report. Inside it, these words are written: "To Miss Agnes Macphail MP, courageous pioneer and untiring worker on behalf of prison reform in Canada. Joseph Archambault."

Her persistence and courage in the face of mean and spiteful attacks had borne fruit. And she didn't stop there. Men and women who had been in prison still came to her for help. Some were worthy causes, some were not, but she listened to them all.

While many praised her for the work she had done on behalf of the prison population, others were ready to blame her when anything went wrong. When prisoners escaped or disturbances happened in jails, it was all Miss Macphail's fault for being "soft on crime." When a policeman was killed by a released convict in Sarnia, Ontario, Agnes received hate mail and threats as if she herself had been responsible for giving the man parole.

But it was obvious to most people that the prisons were in a dire state and that something had to be done. The work program was already in place, and after the Archambault Report came out, the head of the Penitentiaries Board was dismissed.

In the House of Commons, during the debate on the Penitentiaries Commission report, two Conservative members called for an expression of credit to Agnes Macphail for her long fight.

If Agnes felt vindicated, she knew that she could not sit back and consider her job done. A report was all very well, but the implementation of its suggestions would take money and decisiveness on the government's part.

Many years later, the inmates of Canada's penitentiaries still remembered how much Agnes Macphail had helped them. Four years after her death, these words appeared in the Kingston Penitentiary newspaper, the *Telescope*:

> As inmates, most of us are prone to take for granted the privileges we have today...those of us who suffered from day to day and lifted our eyes to "Aggie"...know that it was not always so...
>
> Aggie is dead but lives on in the hearts of countless inmates who knew her and loved her. When the bell tolled for Aggie on February 13, 1954, it tolled for the inmates of every Canadian penitentiary.

James Shaver Woodsworth, Agnes's friend and ally.
A pacifist, he was admired by members of all parties as
"the conscience of the House of Commons."

7

Fighting for Peace

A military band was marching down Front Street in Kingston, leading the parade. The lake was glinting in the sun. The brass instruments shone like gold as the drum major with his baton walked in front, leading them on. Just behind him was a soldier wearing the tiger skin and beating the big bass drum. Children on the sidewalk were imitating the soldiers while their parents looked on with pride.

"It's a splendid sight, isn't it?" a bystander said.

"No, it is not," Agnes Macphail snapped back.

In the House she called the Royal Military College in Kingston, "...a haven for rich kids," a place to "produce snobs" and provide them with "horses, boats, canoes, skis, and a swagger stick..."

When she first went to Ottawa, the First World War had been over for just three years. She had seen the wounded men who came home only to find they were unemployed and penniless. She knew of the thousands who had died, many of them still teenagers. She had met the widows and bereaved mothers.

The war had brought out, in Britain and else-where, a kind of holy belligerence. Women would hand out white feathers, a symbol of cowardice, to young men in civilian clothes whom they saw in the streets without bothering to find out whether these men were soldiers out of uniform or disabled in some way. Patriotic songs were sung everywhere. In church, God was assumed to be on "our" side. Children in schools recited warlike poetry about honour and the glory of dying for your country.

Agnes could only see this as a way to produce a warlike generation. She spoke out strongly – when did she ever speak in any way but strongly! – against cadet groups in schools. The system was educating young people for war instead of peace, and she could see no good in it.

When she felt that what she said was right, she withstood the insults from the other members. But she got into very deep water with her calls for pacifism.

"Why should we take young boys, dress them in uniforms...with their foolish little guns and swords. It is a cowardly thing; it is not a brave thing at all."

Her comments started up a war of words in the House.

"You had better go to Russia."

"Soviet Russian nonsense... "

"If you are a fair example of Canadian womanhood... "

"I think I am."

"I do not think so."

Then she suggested sarcastically that the budget of \$400,000 allotted to cadet groups should be cut by \$399,999, and the money spent on a health program she had drawn up. She planned a system of gymnastic courses in schools, which she felt would ensure that ALL young people were healthy instead of the trained few.

Unwisely, she then went after the sacred and important Empire Day celebrations. The patriotic speeches, the military displays only led to the glorification of war, she said.

She was bitterly attacked for saying, "Mistakenly we stick up silly war memorials all over the place."

For all her sensibility, she couldn't see that with statements like that she was offending veterans as well as all those whose sons and husbands had been killed in the fighting. These people had to believe that their comrades and loved ones had died in a worthy cause. Instead of giving up, she pursued the matter further.

Of course she loved her country, she replied to her accusers, but she hated to see it spending huge sums on what appeared to be preparation for another war. What was the use of Remembrance Day if they didn't remember the horror of war?

To an audience in her home constituency, she said, "I would say to the gun-makers and the cadet-makers, I would say to the people of Canada, 'Whom do you want to kill?'"

In the House of Commons, one member told her that as she had no children, she was unqualified to speak about cadet forces in schools. J.S. Woodsworth, to whom the cause of peace was sacred, stood up to respond. "I have six children," he said to the man, "and am therefore better qualified than you."

The *Ottawa Journal* praised Agnes for her speeches about demilitarizing schools. "Miss Macphail's speech was like a waterfall in the desert."

There were plenty of other people who agreed with her. Times were hard once again in many parts of the country, and the money that was being spent on arms and the military could well have been spent in helping the farmers and the poor in the cities.

Agnes took part in a parade for the No-More-War Society, and the speech she made was taken apart by the *Toronto Telegram* in a way that once again made her appear to be a traitor.

Frustrated that people couldn't see the difference between a desire for friendship between nations and treachery, she went with a group of women on a tour to promote peace.

When the dogs of war in Europe were heard to be growling again, Agnes and J.S. Woodsworth spoke at a large peace rally in Toronto. They hoped that they could get pacifists in Britain to join with them to prevent another bloody conflict.

"No European War for Canadians!" The slogan was seen everywhere. Peace was what people wanted. No one who had seen the terrible destruction of the 1914-18 war could believe it would ever happen again. No one who had read the war memorials that stand in even the smallest towns to list the names of those killed could think of another war. Many of those listed have the same surname, and who could imagine that the sons of those brave men who died would in future be etched on the same block of stone.

In spite of the opposition of Agnes and others, and the feelings of many Canadians, the government began to spend more money on the manufacture of armaments.

"Where is the logic of this outlay of money on guns," she asked, "when half a million people are unemployed. And when in Saskatchewan, schools are closing for lack of funds."

More money, she insisted, should be spent on education and finding jobs. She told the House of a young, trained teacher, unable to find work in a school, earning three dollars a week in a menial job. Another young man was earning a dollar a week as a theatre operator.

"In my generation," she said, "youth did not worry about a job. When I applied for my first job, just to be safe, I applied for five and was accepted in all of them."

Her defence of the young never stopped. When a certain Mr. Pickel delivered a tirade against "today's youth," Agnes replied angrily.

"Youth never serves by following age," she said. "Youth was never finer nor more courageous than it is today; it is adventurous. The young are ready to do and suffer for a better day."

She didn't know, when she spoke those words, how soon the young would be asked to suffer for that "better day."

⚭

In her efforts to keep young people informed, she used to write letters to the teachers in the schools in her area telling them what was going on in Ottawa. They were chatty letters for the teachers to read to their students. She described the goings-on in Parliament and sometimes the glittering social events to which she was invited.

One of these letters nearly brought the House down about her ears.

"Dear Teacher and Pupils," she wrote, "today we will talk about the Chinese War." She went on to describe the awful effects of the drug trade in China, the criminals who kept on making a profit from opium, the Chinese workers who were being exploited. Her letter ended with these words: "We must remember that it is only a few very rich people in England who want to do these dreadful things in China."

Somehow, the Toronto *Globe* got hold of a copy of the letter and printed it.

"Treason!" her opponents in the House shouted. And that was only the beginning of the uproar.

"The letter is full of poisonous untruths."

"Insidious work is being done."

"This is an assault on the minds of the young."

Some Conservative members wanted to have the member for South-East Grey expelled from the House.

The members of the West Coast branch of the Women's Canadian Club added their voice to the outcry, and the premier of Ontario, G. Howard Ferguson, said, "Miss Macphail is trying to shake the loyalty of our young Canadians to the British Empire."

Agnes's future looked very shaky. But she was unrepentant. If only other MPs kept their young constituents so well informed, the whole nation would be better off. The indignant voices were silenced only after two reporters went to Grey County to interview the teacher.

She opened the history textbook and pointed out the paragraphs on the Opium Wars. The facts written there were exactly as Agnes had described. Besides, the teacher said, she liked getting Miss Macphail's letters, and the children enjoyed them too.

A few years later when G. Howard Ferguson was appointed Minister Plenipotentiary in London, Agnes thanked Mackenzie King for arranging it. "It is rather hard on the Court of St. James," she said, "but it is a great relief to the Province of Ontario!"

∞

The next election was called in 1925, four years after her first victory. No one stood against Agnes for the Progressive Party nomination. She visited the separate ridings, made speeches, listened to men and women who came to her for help, and managed to spend a little time with her family.

In October 1925, she defeated the Conservative candidate by more than three thousand votes. She was one of only two members of the Progressive Party elected from Ontario. And she would from now on vote as an Independent.

Mackenzie King had called the election expecting to be returned with a strong majority, but the voices he listened to had been wrong.

The Conservatives had 117 members, the Liberals 101, and the Progressives, 24. Mackenzie King, who lost his own seat in the election, had to try again to get the Progressives to vote with the Liberals. Without them, he had no power. He promised to introduce old-age pensions to win them to his side. They drafted documents on various matters on which they wanted support, the Hudson Bay railway and rural credit among other things.

It was another difficult time for Agnes. One newspaper accused her of selling her vote to the Liberals in return for a job in the cabinet. Like many of the stories written about her, it was untrue. King more than once offered her a place in his government and she always refused.

J.S. Woodsworth used this moment to press for the Pensions Bill. He wrote to the leaders of the other two parties and asked them to enact the Bill. The Conservative leader, Arthur Meighen, stalled. Mackenzie King said yes. The Pensions Bill was passed. It was only a beginning, but it was a moment of triumph for the small group.

A Conservative member, Mr. Stevens, had been investigating stories of a serious crime in the Customs

Department in Quebec. Given their modest salaries, men in that department had been growing rich beyond reason. Smugglers and gangsters were involved. There was an enquiry and a debate in the House.

Well known now as a pacifist, Agnes had been invited to speak at an important conference organized by the Women's International League for Peace and Freedom. It would be a chance to share her ideas with like-minded people.

She was excited. Her first trip to Europe! What was she to wear on the sea voyage? How cold would it be in Denmark? And then, the night before she was to set off, a messenger appeared with "a telegram for Miss Macphail."

It was from the prime minister. He desperately needed her vote in the House. Agnes looked at the pile of clothes on the bed. She thought of the restful time she was going to have on the ship, the speech she was going to make in Dublin. She weighed all this against the loyalty she owed Mackenzie King for his efforts to bring about the Pensions Act and for persuading his government to pass her resolution calling for a work program for people in jail.

She got into a taxi and went to the House of Commons. The transatlantic liner sailed without her.

∽

Then came another vote on the Customs scandal. When Agnes went home to her small flat at night, she was torn in her desire to vote against this affair and her wish to support the Liberals. Some of the Progressives joined with the Conservatives, and they won this time by just two votes.

What happened next is something that political analysts still argue about.

Mackenzie King asked the Governor General to dissolve Parliament. Lord Byng refused. King had to resign. Arthur Meighen happily became prime minister. Mackenzie King fought back. He questioned the right of the Governor General to interfere. He spoke of the inexperience of the new ministers. In a long speech, he asked, "Does Canada always wish to be ruled as a British colony, or does she want to be independent?"

∞

During this time, Agnes was wooed by various suitors, and the Liberals and the Conservatives also came calling. She was a powerful speaker, a significant member of the House. She was a good person to have on your side. Arthur Meighen offered her any cabinet post she wanted except minister of finance if she would join his party – an offer that many would have been unable to refuse whatever their convictions.

It was obvious that the Conservative leader didn't know Agnes Macphail. She would never compromise her principles, all the things she stood for, the farming communities she represented, to sit among men she considered reactionary and, worst of all, militaristic.

She had always resented, she said, the smug and

self-righteous attitude of the Conservatives. "My only satisfaction is that they are now sitting farther off from me."

All the lobbying in the halls and the intrigue made Agnes wish again that there were more women in Parliament because she felt they would have brought a gentler influence to bear.

As the new, very short session of the House opened, she said, "Rumours and counter-rumours have almost destroyed my faith in human nature....The things that are being said, the whisperings going on and the members visiting other members in private rooms are not creditable to Members of this House.... I have come to a place where I almost wish I had gone to Europe the other morning."

Meighen's weak government lasted only three days. Three difficult days. At the next vote, the Progressives voted with the Liberals and Meighen had to resign. It was Dominion Day, July 1, 1926.

Parliament was dissolved and an election called for the following September.

Mackenzie King went to England that fall and helped to put together the Balfour Declaration, which stated that member nations of the Commonwealth were "equal in status, in no way subordinate to one another."

In July of 1926, nomination meetings were held in South-East Grey for the provincial representative of the United Farmers of Ontario. Farquhar Oliver won the vote. He was a family friend and neighbour of the Macphails, and he had helped Agnes in her campaigns. Agnes had encouraged him in his political ambitions, and now she worked for him. They made speeches together at meetings in halls and barns, putting forward their message about tariffs, about relief for the poor. Oliver was only twenty-two. His opponent was Dr. Jamieson, who had represented the riding for many years. Jamieson had been Speaker of the legislature. This was his place and no "boy wonder" was going to take it from him. But with Agnes behind him, the "boy wonder" did just that. Farquhar Oliver was elected to the Ontario legislature.

∞

In her own federal campaign, her Conservative opponent accused Agnes of being a "Liberal in Ottawa." She replied that if a Liberal whip ever tried to tell her what to do, "he would have his head bashed against the wall." Not exactly a proper statement for a pacifist!

Hugh Guthrie came to support her opponent and went off on the red scare tack. "Miss Macphail harbours some doctrines which can only be called Bolshevik in character," he said, hoping to frighten the voters.

The rural population knew Agnes better than this. She was returned as the member for South-East Grey with an even larger majority than before.

But it was a depleted Progressive Party that went to Ottawa that winter. In forty-eight constituencies the Liberals and Progressives had made a deal and only run one candidate. So now, in the House, there were eleven Liberal-Progressives and nine Independent Progessives.

Agnes, who of course remained Independent, was unhappy about these defections from the ranks. She told the Liberal-Progressives that they had a lot to answer for. She accused the Liberal party of being dishonest in promising to follow the Progressive line and failing to do so.

"...I would rather have the bitter, uncompromising, unfriendly and snobbish attitude of the Conservative Party. At least it was honest..."

The Conservatives didn't find this to be a compliment, even a backhanded one.

∽

But there was peace in the land. There was a feeling that good times, if not quite here yet, were just around the corner. The motorcar and the aeroplane were signs that man was conquering distance and even time. The radio was bringing music into every home. The telephone was connecting people together in a new and wonderful way.

Until now, in movie theatres, Rudolph Valentino and the Canadian actresses Marie Dressler and Mary Pickford had held audiences spellbound without speaking a word. Charlie Chaplin and Buster Keaton made audiences shriek with laughter at their silent routines. But with new technology, the "talkies" arrived to add their voices to the cacophony of the new era.

Liquor laws preventing the sale of intoxicating beverages had been enacted in response to the powerful

Temperance organizations. There was still Prohibition in Ontario until 1927; there were gin joints and speakeasies and people were dying from drinking the peculiar brews concocted in illegal stills. Canadian bootleggers were getting rich taking liquor across the St. Lawrence or the Detroit River by boat in the dead of night to the United States, where Prohibition lasted until 1933.

Tuned in to all this, Agnes, learning the new dances of the Jazz Age, was continuing her work on behalf of a better deal for the people she had been elected to represent. And more and more, as time went on, she became a passionate advocate for peace. She would do whatever she could to prevent another generation of young people from being sent overseas to fight.

8

A Dark and Difficult Time

"Why," Agnes asked in the House one day, "should men and women from Russia, from Germany, from Asia feel loyalty to a Royal Family over there in Britain?"

Some of the old gentlemen sitting across the aisle turned purple. One of them shouted, "Traitor!" and others joined in.

But Agnes was only speaking out for the people she saw as she walked to work or when she visited other cities. They were immigrants like her grandparents, but many of them came from countries where the language and customs were very different from those in Canada. In the bakery, the Italian woman behind the counter wished her "Buon giorno." The Polish man in

National Archives of Canada/PA-126949

William Lyon Mackenzie King addressing the crowd at
celebrations of the Diamond Jubilee of Confederation.
Prime minister for most of her years in Parliament,
he wooed Agnes for his Party but never won her over.

the delicatessen offered her a taste of kielbasa and Agnes learned to say "Tak" when she accepted it.

∞

Whenever Agnes Macphail, MP walked into the House of Commons and took in the rich wood panelling, the green upholstered seats, the Speaker's chair, the table with all its history, she was proud to be part of the government of her country, and she was a patriot, even if her outspoken views led people to think otherwise.

She tried her best to fight against the narrow outlook of some of her colleagues and persuade them to consider the lives of all the different kinds of people who had come from elsewhere.

"We should teach history," she said, "in such a way that the child would realize that neither Britain, the United States, nor Canada has a corner on the progress of the human race."

∞

Her words often fell on stony ground in the House, but there were others who appreciated them as she continued to speak out loudly on behalf of farmers, women, immigrants, and anyone else whom she felt was not getting a fair deal.

The *Ottawa Journal* wrote, "Miss Macphail has wit, satire, humour, and a parliamentary manner which would delight a Lloyd George."

During the summer recess she was invited to take part in the culture tours that were named "Chautauqua" after the town in New York State where they had begun decades earlier. Chautauqua was a highly organized travelling circus of talks, readings, music hall acts, and concerts. These events, which took place in tents, church halls, and schools, brought a week of excitement and stimulation to many small towns and villages in rural parts of Canada. Crowds of people who couldn't afford to go to a nearby city looked forward for months to the arrival of Chautauqua.

In 1928, Agnes went on a ten-week tour of western Canada. It wasn't easy going. Often, after an evening lecture, she would have to move on to the next town and would sometimes arrive in the middle of the night to find the small hotel closed up. But local people were delighted to receive the speakers and musicians, the actors and magicians, into their homes and to make them welcome.

It hardly seemed like a good way for a busy woman to spend her vacation, but Agnes needed the money. The forty-five-dollar navy blue dress she had worn to the opening of Parliament in her first session was long gone. She enjoyed shopping for clothes and she had not lost her habit of buying expensive gifts. When she entertained her friends in the House of Commons dining room, she did so lavishly.

Everywhere she went she drew a large audience. Her style was her own. At times conversational, at times demagogic, she held her listeners enthralled, waiting for her next sharp comment. Toronto's *Saturday Night Magazine* described her as, "Strong, intellectual, shrewd, and aggressive. A speaker of distinct ability."

She was able to spread her views to many provinces. She talked about the unequal tariff system, about education, about life in Parliament. When she spoke about equality between the sexes, she sometimes berated women for not making more of an effort to move to higher places in business, politics, and other largely male preserves. The phantom footsteps of women who would follow her into Parliament were still exactly that. Only one other woman had become an MP after her. What were the rest doing?

It was briefly a time of prosperity and there seemed to be no need to protest and to move forward. Many women were doing remarkable voluntary work, but few were boldly reaching for the top jobs.

As she travelled, Agnes carried with her the notes for her next lecture as well as papers and letters so that she could keep on working for her constituents.

She had never been a pork-barrel politician but the township of Durham had been wanting a post office for twenty years. And for twenty years, politicians had been promising the people a post office but no post office had been delivered. Agnes pressed the matter, and, as a reward for her support, Mackenzie King finally granted this small wish. Agnes had hoped to be able to ceremoniously open this long-awaited benefit to her constituents, but that part of her request was denied.

She was still writing a weekly letter to her home newspaper. Sometimes the letter described the social life in the capital. There were balls and dinners and receptions, and Agnes, with her lively ways and witty talk, was a popular guest.

The twenties were high and low years for Agnes and for Canada. Jazz, movies, new and wonderful home appliances, cars, and most of all, peace, gave people the feeling that life was great and could only get better. But, as is often the case in good times, the seeds of disaster were there for those who could see. Not many were looking.

∞

It was 1927, the year of Canada's Diamond Jubilee, and it was time for a sixtieth birthday party. Mackenzie King named Agnes to his committee to oversee the plans for a big celebration. Was Agnes pleased? No! She asked at once for her name to be withdrawn.

"Looking over the names here," she said to the prime minister, "I see that they do not belong to my class, and unless I can go in as one of my own people, I would not care to go in at all."

Besides, there were, she pointed out, only Anglo-Saxon Canadian names among the chosen.

Mackenzie King asked her to wait an hour or two. Later that evening, he added four other people to the committee: the president of the Labour Congress; a French-Canadian; a man of European extraction; the head of the Teachers' Federation.

Agnes had once more made her point and won.

∞

Now came something more serious. On behalf of Canada, Mackenzie King had signed the Kellogg-Briand Pact, a multilateral treaty for the renunciation of war.

Agnes was pleased, but she wanted to go further and once again brought up the matter of military spending. In 1929, the estimates for defence spending were 20 million dollars. "What sense does this make," she asked, "when sixty-two nations of the world have signed a peace treaty? Our military colleges and schoolbooks reek with the glorification of war. During our celebrations we trot out our military people possibly because their coats are bright."

She put forward a resolution for educational methods that would promote peace. The Industrial and International Relations Committee conducted an enquiry into the matter, but that was as far as it went.

It was in 1929 that she finally made her European trip. Mackenzie King invited her to go as a delegate to the League of Nations in Geneva. Agnes was never one to say "thank you" without checking into the details. She had the habit of looking every gift horse in the mouth. "Interested if all parties are represented," she telegraphed to Mr. King. "If it is to be an all-Liberal group, I will stay at home."

Only when she was assured that members of all parties were included did she begin to pack.

She went first to Prague, to a meeting of the Women's International League. Thrilled to be in this ancient city, she walked on the cobbled streets and went up Hradcany hill to look at the castle and the ancient cathedral where the Kings of Bohemia had been crowned.

From Prague, she went to Geneva. She could have spent days admiring the lake and gazing at the Alps beyond. But there was serious work to be done.

Agnes saw the League of Nations as an important way to world peace, and she had high hopes for its influence in the world. In 1929, it had already been in existence for ten years, and it brought together the representatives of many different countries. When she went into the meeting room, she carried with her her strong desire for the total abolition of war. She was the first woman delegate and was – naturally, because of her sex – assigned to the Health and Welfare Committee! Annoyed, she asked to be put on the Disarmament Committee instead, and was.

She made herself unpopular with the other delegates from Canada because she was more careful over her travelling costs than if she had been spending her own money. Her colleagues, enjoying a European trip at the taxpayers' expense, resented being shown up by the only woman present.

Coming home meant coming down to earth with a thud. In October that year, the stock market crashed and fortunes were lost overnight. This disaster shook the financial world to its roots, and the rest of the world felt the aftershock. If the rich and powerful were not secure, what would happen to everyone else?

It was the beginning of a dark and difficult time.

∞

Agnes herself was soon concerned with a personal tragedy. In January 1930, Dougald Macphail, her beloved father, died. He was sixty-five and had been in the new brick house he had planned for so long only five years. Agnes mourned this man deeply. He had always looked out for his daughter, always sought the best for her. Their arguments had been forceful but short. They had never failed to kiss and make up. Though he had not encouraged her to begin her parliamentary career, he read her speeches, her letters, and spoke proudly of his clever child.

She returned to Ottawa deeply saddened, worried about her bereaved mother, and just in time to face the trials of a new election.

∞

Mackenzie King had responded to the growing problems in the country in a penny-pinching way. He made a statement he would soon regret. He would not give more money to the provinces, he said, because they would only use it for "alleged unemployment purposes."

"I would not give a cent to any Tory government," he stated.

From across the aisle, R.B. Bennett shouted, "Shame!"

Mr. Stevens echoed, "Shame!"

Mr. King asked, "Do my honourable friends say, 'Shame'?"

R.B. Bennett replied, "Yes, shame."

"What is there to be ashamed of?" asked King.

"You ought to be ashamed of that," Stevens answered.

"I would not give them a five-cent piece," King replied.

He was so sure of winning the next election that he felt he could make such statements with impunity. Agnes and others knew that words like those could have very damaging consequences.

R.B. Bennett, the leader of the Conservatives, was a westerner portrayed in cartoons as fat and bald and bespectacled. As indeed he was. But he promised to open up trade and to be more generous to the provinces than King had been.

∞

This federal election in 1930 was the first one in which the new wireless radio had an effect. Some of the early sets in their fine wooden cabinets cost as much as a car. Others were home-made affairs with wires sticking out all over the place. Soon there was a radio of one kind or another in nearly every home. People tuned in to comedy shows from the States, and on Saturday evenings, *Hockey Night in Canada* held families spellbound. And politicians like Mackenzie King and R.B. Bennett were able to broadcast their campaign promises directly into people's living rooms.

Before long, King's "not a five-cent piece" phrase came back to haunt him. He was shown up as a man who didn't care about the growing number of unemployed men and women in the country.

The Conservative party won a with a large majority, 137 seats. King's Liberals had only 91 seats. The Progressives won 12. This time there were six female candidates in the race, but Agnes Macphail was the only one elected.

∞

William Lyon Mackenzie King was prime minister for fourteen of Agnes Macphail's nineteen years in Parliament. That he respected and admired her is shown in the way he offered her posts in his cabinet and appointed her to committees. He was interested in labour affairs as she was, but he took a ponderous approach to the country's problems, and his various governments moved too slowly.

R.B. Bennett, the new prime minister, was charming to Agnes outside the House of Commons, and she enjoyed his company. But inside the House his beliefs and his way of dealing with the country's problems caused many a fight between them.

In 1929, wheat farmers on the Prairies were earning 250 million dollars from their product. Ontario and Quebec farmers, though they had less than half the productive land, were also thriving. Their products – livestock, fruit, vegetables, tobacco – were of higher value. More cars and mechanized farm machinery meant there was less need for horses, less need for oats and hay. But demand for food from the growing population in the cities meant that Ontario farms were prospering – for a time.

The Conservatives took charge at a difficult time. In 1931, Ontario farmers' receipts had shrunk by 50 per cent, a terrible drop in income. They had not suffered from drought as the western farmers had, but because there was so little money in people's pockets, they had no market for their dairy products. Teachers in rural schools were sometimes paid in kind, with vegetables, wood for their fires, or clothing. There was often, simply, no cash.

Agnes, like many others, wanted better methods of distributing goods and money. She saw co-operatives as being the way of the future; the only way that people could thrive was to avoid the costs of marketing and share the profits fairly.

When W. Eggleston, a journalist, called Agnes a "militant agrarian," she probably did not take this as an insult because, in a way, it's exactly what she was.

The Depression now in full swing was affecting different kinds of people in all parts of the country. Bennett, like a deer caught in the headlights, seemed unable to move forward. He established "relief" camps for single men but did nothing to create real work. Gasoline had become scarce, and people called the cars drawn by horses that they saw on the city streets "Bennett buggies."

In the West it was the drought that destroyed the farms; in the East it was poverty and unemployment. People had no money to spend on milk and meat. For many, food, like clothes, had become a luxury.

By 1933, nearly a third of the population was unemployed. In Saskatchewan, it was two-thirds. The worst hit were farmers, young people, and small business operators. Many of the immigrants Agnes had spoken out for were being sent back to their own countries because there was no work for them in Canada.

People went from place to place looking desperately for jobs of any kind. Men and women who previously would not have dreamed of begging were now on the street, panhandling. Factories were closing. People without money to spend cannot go shopping, and a downward spiral was created. If people don't buy goods, the manufacture of goods declines; people are laid off, and with less money to spend, they buy even less.

At that time there was no unemployment insurance. The federal government thought the provinces should look after their own poor, and because of this many families fell between the cracks.

It wasn't only members of the CCF who saw the need for change. As many leaders do when election time draws near, R.B. Bennett, copying President Roosevelt's New Deal in the United States, proposed some sweeping reforms. He would now consider doing something about the rights of labour and would also increase the purchasing power of the people.

Agnes called these reforms "five years too late." But it showed, she said, the rising power of the CCF. Bennett's policies, she said, had driven people to support the new party.

"The Canadian people," she stated, "cannot be reconciled to continued want and privation, suffering and disease, and an early death in a land of abundance."

Bennett, who was never one to underestimate himself, said, "If the system needs changing, I will change it."

Agnes wanted to know what the farmers were going to get out of Bennett's "new deal," which seemed to her to be weighted once again in favour of industry.

"The farmers were here first," she said. "They were the pioneers who cleared the land and opened up the West; let us not now serve them last."

One of the proposed reforms caused an argument between Agnes and her longtime friend J.S. Woodsworth: the law to give workers an eight-hour day.

Woodsworth, who might have known better, said that farmers should organize and work two shifts, perhaps three, "as they do in industry."

Agnes jumped on this. She knew how hard the farmer's life was. Often the farmer and his wife and children worked all the daylight hours just to make a simple living.

"The farmers could no more think of putting on double and treble shifts than flying to the moon!

"They know a little bit more about hard work and about saving than any other large group of people; ... they are the bedrock of our whole national life..."

The newspapers praised her, and in her home constituency they saw that their Aggie was sticking up for them once more. But Mackenzie King gloated at what he saw as a division in the CCF. He wanted to poach more of its members for the Liberals as he began to campaign again.

He had been active as Opposition leader, and when election time came, the voters rallied to the Liberal cry of "King or Chaos."

By 1935, the voters were fed up with both the major political parties, who had failed to relieve the suffering caused by the Great Depression. All the same, voters were afraid of the new party and its far-reaching ideas, and its opponents continued to call the CCF-ers "communists."

∽

"Come in and sit down, Aggie." Her old neighbour in Ceylon was offering the MP for the area a cup of tea after a hard day of canvassing. "Take the weight off your feet."

Agnes heard a sound from the other room, and in came a group of women bearing a gift for her. It was a beautiful handmade quilt. Agnes was touched and very grateful for their support and affection.

Everywhere she went, constituents treated her in a kindly, familiar way. They knew how hard she worked on their behalf. But Agnes Macphail knew this was to be a more difficult election. She had to campaign hard. The boundaries of the constituency had been changed, and she had to explain herself and her ideas to new voters, many of whom were staunch Liberals.

Unlike many other politicians, she wasn't about to water down any of her ideas to please anyone or simply to win votes. She plainly laid out her policies for the future, little knowing what that future might bring.

R.B. Bennett, prime minister of Canada 1930-1935. A friend to
Agnes outside the House but a strong opponent inside. He
rarely won their arguments.

9

The Gathering Clouds

"Re-elect Agnes Macphail. For fourteen years I have endeavoured to render faithful and enterprising service." So said the posters scattered round the electoral district now named Grey-Bruce.

"A vote for Agnes Macphail is a wasted vote," responded her opponents. "The power is with the two main parties."

To her farming audiences, Agnes spoke about the problems of transporting livestock. The days were long gone when herds of cattle could be moved on foot along the highway to the towns. Now it was a question of whether the railways or trucks were more economical, and both appeared to be charging too much.

To the town people she spoke about the need for better roads. Motorcars were becoming cheaper and more and more of them were being driven on roads that had been meant for horse-drawn carts.

In Priceville, she defended her views at a "political ice cream social" and made it clear that she would continue as she had begun, to speak out first and foremost on behalf of farmers.

∞

In October 1935 another Election Day arrived. The candidates waited as the ballot papers were counted by hand. It was expected to be a close-run affair and few were making bets on the outcome.

The Liberal and Conservative candidates were running neck and neck as the night went on, but gradually Agnes gained on them, and with 7,210 votes she won her fifth election.

R.B. Bennett with his imitation "New Deal" had lost the country's confidence. His plans for helping the poor and the unemployed were too late and too little and were seen to favour industry over other groups, especially farmers.

The Parliament that met in 1936 was distinctly Liberal, with only 39 Conservatives in Opposition. The CCF won 7 seats and there were 17 Social Credit members and 11 Others. With a powerful majority, Mackenzie King must now see what he could do to sort out the problems of a country still suffering from the ravages of the Great Depression.

Agnes went back to Ottawa with all the confidence of a longtime member of the House. She had changed greatly from the simply dressed woman who had made her way into the House of Commons in 1921. She was a distinctive figure now as she strode about Ottawa, her long cape around her shoulders. She wore a pince-nez, which gave her a learned look. In the evenings, she often wore black outfits with silver jewellery. Her hair was curly. And she was proud of her slender hands and narrow feet. She was an elegant woman with a "deep and lovely" voice. Wherever she went, she was a presence.

Neither she nor Mackenzie King nor most of the MPs foresaw the terrible decision they would have to make in a few short years.

Agnes had recovered from the awful trials of the Charles Baynes affair. And now as well as prison reform there were many other issues to deal with. To some of her colleagues she appeared to be like a child with a huge Santa Claus list. Her wish list included:

- a real health insurance scheme
- subsidized housing
- scholarships for students
- an increase in Old Age Pensions
- pensions for the blind.

When the pension bill for the blind was passed, she went on to fight for pensions for the disabled.

"And who is to pay for all these social programs?" she was asked in debate.

She replied, "There are some birds of passage, rather wealthy birds, who fly to the Bahamas. One of them is Mr. Harry Oakes and he is justifying his flight in order that he might avoid taxes."

It was all right for those birds of passage to move away, she said, but they should be made to return some of their wealth to the country that had made them rich. It was a sentiment shared by many, but nothing was done to change the rules. The very wealthy who chose to do so went on transferring their money out of the country to avoid paying taxes in Canada.

A man who was soon to become Governor of the Bahamas was much in the news just then. King George V died, and his eldest son, the Prince of Wales, became King Edward VIII. Like a prince in a fairy tale, he had fallen in love with a woman who was considered unsuitable to be his Queen. Wallis Warfield Simpson was a divorced woman and an American. Many people were clamouring for Edward to renounce her or give up the throne.

Agnes had something to say about this affair, too.

"The romance of King Edward the Eighth and Mrs. Simpson should not be shattered," she said. Although a lot of people felt as she did, it made no difference. There was so much pressure from the Church of England and from many politicians at Westminster that the new King, choosing love over a crown, had to go. He became the Duke of Windsor, and his younger brother George became King in his place. In parts of Canada sympathy for the couple was so strong that after the abdication, a headline in a Toronto paper read, "Duke of Windsor for Prime Minister."

෩

The Great Depression had given Canadians so much to think about at home that the gathering storms in Europe still seemed very far off. "Hitler kills hundreds," said the papers. Canadians read the stories but most of them were paying more attention to the after-effects of drought on the Prairies than the increasing power of the Nazis in Germany, which seemed to have little connection to their lives in Canada.

Agnes, like many others, was still involved in peace movements. She had been excited by the formation of the League of Nations and proud to be a member of it, but she felt that it had failed to solve the problem of disarmament.

There were so many reminders of the last war around – the ex-soldiers who had been gassed and were permanent invalids, the widows who kept the photographs of their young husbands on the dresser and who were struggling to bring up children on their own, the war memorials – that it was hard to believe that sane and civilized people could allow this to happen all over again.

Mackenzie King talked of neutrality. Hitler was building up his army, but Germany was far away. If, by chance, there should be war in Europe, then Canada was going to stay out of it. If people over there wanted to fight, let them. It was a sentiment shared by many in North America, not only the pacifists. At the same time, though, the government was increasing the amount of money it spent on the manufacture of guns and war machines.

"We are not concerned with aggression," Mackenzie King said, defending his rearmament policy. "We are concerned with the defence of Canada."

∞

There was plenty to worry about at home. Young people as well as older ones were suffering from lack of work. Farmers were being forced to give up their farms, and desperate men were still travelling from place to place willing to do anything in order to earn a little money.

Agnes grew angry with the Liberal government, which she felt was doing no more to help the unemployed than R.B. Bennett's Conservatives had done in the five years before. It was like struggling with Jell-O, and sometimes, in spite of her allies in the House, Agnes felt she was struggling alone.

∞

It was a time of personal disappointments as well, and of bereavement. Farquhar Oliver, the young friend and neighbour Agnes had brought into politics and whose career she had nurtured, was moving to the right. He had come under the influence of Mitchell Hepburn, the Conservative premier of Ontario, a man Agnes despised. When Hepburn sent tanks to put down a strike in Ottawa, Agnes called him a fascist and a "tin-pot Mussolini." She was sad to see her young friend going, as she saw it, entirely in the wrong direction.

She was invited in 1936 to go on a tour of Scandinavia and Russia. Denmark especially impressed her. She admired the way the socialist democracies worked. She felt that people had more say in their government there than they did in other countries, and that the population had more in the way of social benefits. In Russia she found the people to be unhappy-looking, tired, drab. She had seen the grass on the other side of the fence, and while some of it was lush and green, some was a much less desirable colour. She was, she said when she got back, happier than ever to be a Canadian.

Well-travelled, knowledgeable, Agnes had become a popular speaker across the border. On misty mornings or dark evenings, a train would pull into a city station. An onlooker would have seen two women walking slowly towards each other along a railway platform. They were strangers, but each of them knew at once who the other was. The smart woman who had just stepped down from the train carrying a suitcase was Agnes Macphail, and the person coming towards her was a smiling, well-dressed woman wearing the latest thing in hats. Agnes knew she would say something like, "We're so glad you've come to speak to our group. We have just an hour before you go on. Would you care to freshen up? A cup of tea perhaps?"

At times, all the people who came to greet her looked like the same person, and all the station platforms were one platform. She knew this was Chicago because it was Tuesday. Yesterday it had been Flint, tomorrow or the day after it would be Minneapolis. America was a confusing blur of fields and towns that moved by her carriage window.

Harold Peat, an American, had invited Agnes to join his list of eminent touring lecturers. Also on the list were the British MP, Winston Churchill; the philosopher, Bertrand Russell; and the famous author, H.G.Wells. Peat described Agnes Macphail in his advertisements as "a humanist whose lance is courage and foresight."

The tours were just as rigorous as Chautauqua was. In one three-week trip she spoke in Chicago, Minneapolis, Flint, Sioux City, Omaha, Yankton, and several other places.

In Baton Rouge, Louisiana, she asked the audience to consider the question, "Can democracy survive?" and she met the notorious governor of the state, Huey Long.

"Is he interested in the condition of the masses or in power for himself?" she asked.

"In the masses," an indignant supporter replied.

Agnes pointed out that Long's methods of getting his way, with violence and skulduggery, were hardly democratic.

"He fights fire with fire," she was told.

In Long's view, Canada was a place of no importance that should be annexed to the States. Later that same year, he was assassinated, but not, as far as is known, for his opinion of Agnes Macphail's beloved country.

The lectures paid well, and Agnes, still incurably generous to others, needed the money. She always had heavy expenses and was now helping to support her mother.

She was in the States on a speaking tour in 1937 when she received word that her mother was very ill. She returned to Ceylon at once to spend time nursing her. In those few weeks, sitting beside her mother, tending to her, talking about the hardships her grandparents, John and Jean Campbell, had endured in their first years in their new country, Agnes came to understand Henrietta's love. This stern woman had never offered many words of praise and encouragement to her daughter, but in different ways their lives were similar. Both had overcome difficulties, had worked hard without complaint and without compromise. And when death came, Agnes knew she had lost a mother who, if she had said little, had understood and loved her.

Her sisters, Gertha and Lilly, and her nieces and friends all were there with support and consolation, but this new loss left Agnes desolate. She was alone.

∞

She went back to work and continued to pound away at the barriers that still kept women from certain jobs. It was, as she saw it, often the ingrained attitude of both sexes that kept women "in their place." She knew that if only more women could be elected to Parliament, laws would be enacted much more quickly.

∞

She made sure that her constituents were her first priority. *The Toronto Star* said, "She cultivates her political garden but it is because she really likes gardening." This was a way of saying that Agnes looked after the people in Grey-Bruce not only because she wanted their votes but because she understood their needs and truly wanted to help them.

∽

In 1938, when Hitler's army marched on Czechoslovakia and Austria, everyone's eyes turned to Europe. Could Hitler be stopped? Should he be given these small territories to make up for the – as some saw it – "unfair" treatment Germany had received after the last war? Later that year, when Neville Chamberlain, the British prime minister, returned from a meeting with Hitler in Munich and declared that there would be "peace in our time," many sighed with relief.

Whether Chamberlain was buying time so that Britain could better prepare for war or whether he believed Hitler's words is a matter for debate. But those who knew saw that war was inevitable.

In May the following year, when many were still hoping for peace, King George VI and Queen Elizabeth arrived in Ottawa on a royal tour. They were to unveil the million-dollar war memorial, built to honour the dead of the last war.

Agnes learned how to curtsey, to put one leg behind the other and bend her knee and bow her head, and she was honoured to be presented to their majesties. She didn't mention her support of the Duke and Mrs. Simpson.

Meeting the royal couple was only one VIP event in that busy year. She was invited along with other distinguished guests to board a Trans-Canada Airlines plane for the first-ever cross-country flight. That was to be, in more ways than one, the high point of her career.

She had achieved much in her years in Parliament, but there was still much to do and she planned to spend the rest of her working life in Ottawa doing it. She found a larger apartment and wrote to a neighbour in Ceylon, "Now I need some things. The spread Mother gave me, the one that is now in the front room....three knives with white handles and forks to match...tablecloths, especially the one with a lot of green in it."

There would be dinners, parties, and she would have her own comfortable home. But it was not about to be a comfortable time.

She was in her old friend J.S. Woodsworth's office one day. They had worked hard together to achieve so much – prison reform, a better deal for workers – and they had helped to found a new party. They were true comrades.

But now he was frowning at her, asking her seriously, "Am I going to have to take your picture off the wall, Aggie?"

She shook her head but couldn't answer him.

Woodsworth had photographs on his office wall of people he admired, politicians and others who worked for peace and for the rights of working men and women.

"I've had to take Ramsay Macdonald down," he told her. Macdonald, the British Labour leader, had, Woodsworth felt, betrayed the cause by throwing his lot in with the Conservatives. Now he feared that Agnes was walking away from her pacifist principles.

"Does this mean you won't want me beside you?" she asked.

She had been regularly sitting with him and helping with his notes because his eyes were growing weaker. He smiled at her. They would remain friends.

☙

Seeing the events in Europe, the behaviour of Hitler and his henchmen, Agnes had begun to realize that there was no course left open to the nation but to join in the fight against the Nazi evil. She was sad to leave her old friend to stand alone, but as always, she had to vote as her conscience dictated.

☙

When Parliament assembled on September 7, 1939 to consider a formal Declaration of War, Agnes was deeply unhappy. She had seen it all before and had for so long fought against this tragedy, and here it was happening again.

In her speech to the House, she spoke out one more time for the farmers. "They have been paying for the last war ever since it ended." she said. "Let us not sacrifice agriculture to defence again."

☙

Woodsworth stuck to his beliefs and said, "I suggest that the common people of the country gain nothing by slaughtering the common people of any other country..."

Mackenzie King paid tribute to Woodsworth and his beliefs. "But," he went on, "…when it comes to a fight between good and evil, if we do not destroy the evil, it is going to destroy all that there is of good."

Ernest Lapointe said, "These are indeed grave and solemn circumstances. Every speech that has been made here shows that this will be a gigantic conflict."

A few days later, in a hushed and solemn chamber, the House was asked to vote for peace or war. After the votes were counted, the grim words were spoken: "A state of war with the German Reich exists as of the tenth day of September 1939."

Agnes had dreaded this moment. She who had fought so long for peace had voted for war. Given the tragedies happening in Europe, the obvious aggression, she couldn't do otherwise. But it was an awful day and, as she well knew, a fatal day for some of those boarding the troopships that would carry them to the battlefields of France and places yet unknown.

∽

J.S. Woodsworth resigned as leader of the CCF. He was so strongly opposed to Canada having any part in a new war that he couldn't belong to a party that supported the government. He was and always remained a pacifist.

∽

In January 1940, the Ontario government passed a resolution denouncing the federal government's conduct of the war. Because of this, Mackenzie King was able to dissolve Parliament and call an election for March 25th.

March in rural Ontario! Agnes knew it would be difficult for farmers to get out on winter roads and told the prime minister so, but the date was set.

With her solid record in Parliament, her many loyal supporters, and her international reputation as a fine speaker, Agnes Macphail could hit the wintry campaign trail with confidence and a solid program. The farmers needed protection against the industrialists, against those who wanted to conscript them into the army. The rights of prisoners and ex-convicts had to be upheld. Young people had to be protected from those politicians who wanted to skimp on money for education. Old people needed larger pensions. The country must set up a decent health service so that no child should die because his parents could not afford to pay for an appendix operation.

Agnes Macphail knew there was much to be done, and she would return to Ottawa to do it.

10

Still So Much to Do

Ceylon, Ontario. Election Day, 1940

Agnes Macphail, now a fifty-year-old woman with wavy white hair, stood looking out of the farmhouse window in despair.

"Look at all that snow," she said. "I told him. I told Mackenzie King this would happen."

Many of the roads in the area were blocked by twelve-foot drifts. "Who will risk their cars or horses on a day like this?"

She'd worked hard but the campaign had been difficult. Here they were in the middle of another war, and at every meeting, her opponents reminded the voters of her pacifist views.

Agnes Macphail and Ted Jolliffe at the 1948 CCF convention.

Working to the end for the causes she believed in,
she always had time for friends and family.

"Agnes Macphail said we should spend no money on arms."

"Agnes Macphail said we should close down the Military College."

Worst of all, they called her "traitor."

She'd quarreled with her executive committee about the way they were running her campaign and now, again, she was blaming the prime minister for setting an election date in winter.

But as she stood there by the window, she couldn't believe that the voters would let her down. Unlike her opponent in that first election twenty years before, she had not been silent. Her work on behalf of her constituents was well known. Somehow, the votes would be there.

Later that evening, her family and friends sat in the living room and waited. The counting of votes seemed dreadfully slow. Finally, the results were in. The unthinkable had happened. Agnes Campbell Macphail, with only 4,000 votes, had lost to the young Liberal candidate, Walter Harris.

The Conservatives had the same number of seats as before, 39, and the Liberals were back in power with a huge majority, 178. The CCF returned only eight members; the remaining seats were won by the Social Credit Party and Others.

Agnes was devastated. She was hurt and angry and, for a time, bitter.

The press, as usual, was quick to respond. One headline read, "The Passing of Agnes Macphail," as if she had died. In fact, she had lost what had become life to her: her place at the centre of her country's affairs.

All the letters and tributes she received did nothing to help.

One admirer said, "I think every woman in Canada owes you a debt of gratitude."

Agnes sharply replied, "In that case they should have voted for me."

It's not easy to live on gratitude. She now needed not only work but money. She had always feared being poor in her old age. She fought for pensions for others but had none herself. She owned the house in Ceylon but had no income to pay for its upkeep.

She approached old friends in her search for a job, but it was wartime and people had other things on their minds. In her depressed state, Agnes did not present herself well in interviews.

She was still a political figure of consequence, and speaking engagements came her way, but these did not bring in enough to live on. What was she to do?

The future she had planned for herself in her new home in Ottawa, at the centre of political life, had floated away like a balloon. "Am I to sit in my house in rural Ontario and make jam? Take up quilting?" she asked.

It was an echo of the question she had asked herself thirty years before when she lay in bed ill and filled with fear that she would never work again. Slowly, just as she had then, as her mother had taught her, she picked herself up as well as she could and moved on.

The leader of the Ontario branch of the CCF asked her to become the provincial organizer for the party. It was a comedown for Agnes Macphail, MP, the woman who had once been called a future prime minister. But she drew on the strength of will she had inherited from her Scottish grandparents, put her foot down on the pedal of her Ford car, and drove round the familiar territory to speak about the Party to rural audiences and to recruit new members. When funds ran low and the Party was no longer able to pay her, she continued to do the work for a nominal sum.

John Foote, the Minister of Reform Institutions, asked her to go on a trip to look at a progressive reform institution in West Virginia. On her return, she was invited to speak about her experiences at a Unitarian Church in Toronto. Her moving speech affected many of the women in the audience. They responded to her attitude to the unfortunate prisoners: There but for the grace of God, goes Agnes Macphail.

From this meeting grew the beginnings of the Elizabeth Fry Society, which helped and still helps women who have been released from jail as well as those who remain in prison.

She gave speeches at schools and clubs and churches, to farmers' groups and ratepayers' gatherings, the YWCA, and the Civil Liberties Association. She promoted her old causes and asked questions about new ones. "Rural education. Does it meet present-day needs?" was one of her topics. She who had been a teacher in small country schools saw the need for young people to expand their horizons and to go beyond the farm fence if they wanted to compete in the new, fast world of the future.

A large, comfortable house was for rent on St. Clair Avenue in Toronto. Agnes moved in and gathered a few congenial women to share it with her. She hired a cook and a maid, and with her friends around her, she enjoyed a kind of communal living that gave her a base of support.

Offers of work began to come her way, but nothing that would bring in enough money for her to live on.

The editor of *The Globe and Mail* asked her to write a column under the heading "Farm Betterment." The pieces, written in her sharp speaking style, were about her continuing concerns for the welfare of the farmers. She wrote about her life on the farm in Proton Township, about the problems of marketing livestock, about the ongoing unfairness of the protective tariff.

One day, the editor invited her to have lunch with him. "I want," he said, "to set up a committee to speed up the Canadian war effort. It is all too slow. Will you join me, Miss Macphail?"

Agnes looked at him across the table. He was a man she respected, but he was asking her to compromise her principles. Yes, she had voted for the Declaration of War, but she couldn't bring herself to do something that would mean sending more young men overseas or building more war machinery.

Her last column appeared shortly afterwards, and that source of income dried up too.

ᙯ

For a moment the House of Commons seemed to be opening its great doors to her again. Was it possible that she might once more represent a farming constituency in Parliament and sit in that fine chamber?

W.G. Brown, the member for Saskatoon, had died, and there was a vacancy. Brown had believed that it was possible to work with the Communists to achieve common goals. The chairman of the United Reform Party asked Agnes to stand in his place.

She went to Saskatchewan and campaigned, but she found it difficult to consider working with people who held to the Communist party line. She was perhaps relieved when she lost the election to the Conservative, Alfred H. Bence, who was the tennis champion of the province.

Her doctor told her to take a vacation, and she made a trip out West to see old friends and to get away from her struggle to make ends meet. But she couldn't relax when she knew that London was being bombed and that men and women and children were being killed, not only there but all over Europe. Unrested, she returned home to look once again for work.

∽

In 1943, Agnes was asked to run as the CCF candidate for York East in the Ontario provincial election. This was a very different constituency from her old Grey-Bruce riding. It was urban and heavily populated. The voters were dependent on industry rather than farming for their livelihoods. People were skeptical of her chances. The *Toronto Telegram* wrote about her dismissively as it often had before. In spite of the newspaper's comments about her politics and her gender, Agnes won the seat. She was back among the lawmakers.

The CCF with thirty-four members became the official Opposition in the Ontario legislature at Queen's Park in Toronto.

In 1944 when the session began, Agnes was there to make her presence felt. The Queen's Park Chamber was small and much less imposing than the one she had been used to in Ottawa. Moreover, the Conservative government was led by George Drew, a man she never liked. He was against nearly everything Agnes Macphail stood for, and for the next two years she had an ongoing battle with him. She fought, as always, fiercely, for the rights of those who were underprivileged, especially the elderly. She could have been speaking about herself when she attacked Drew's government, saying, "We have no welfare, no visiting people, no counsellors for pensioners.... We have done nothing at all to make them feel that the end of life is good."

When 1945 brought peace and the hope of a new, better world, Agnes joined in the celebrations. The soldiers would return, families would be reunited. Like everyone else in the country, Agnes hoped that life would be easier.

If she stayed on as a member of the Ontario legislature, the salary would at least pay her living expenses.

But the leader of the CCF, E.B. Jolliffe, chose that moment to accuse George Drew of employing a separate police force to spy on organized labour, on unions. This was a shocking charge to make. If true, it meant that Drew was using the police force for political ends. A commission was set up to find out the facts. Jolliffe's accusation was dismissed.

Drew was able to use the matter against the CCF in the next election. Support for the party shrank, and only eight members were returned to the legislature. Agnes was not among them.

∽

The Second World War had changed the way people viewed the world. Agnes, with her talk of rural life and the price of wheat, appeared to be out of step. Many people still believed that the world, and their part of it, in particular, would be wonderful and new with the coming of peace. Agnes's warnings of difficult times ahead were not what voters wanted to hear.

In the same year, the landlord sold the St. Clair house. Agnes and her friends had to go their separate ways and find other places to live.

She returned to Ceylon. The strain of her struggles was beginning to tell on her health, and she suffered a slight stroke. Doctors again told her to take time out. She went to Mexico, where she admired the ancient ruins and read the country's history, but, she wrote home, "I cannot easily sit around doing nothing when there is still so much to do."

She came back to Canada unrested and decided to share a home in Toronto with her friend Ruby Campbell.

In all her busy political life, her travelling, and the difficulties of these years, Agnes had the comfort and support of her family. Her sisters and nieces were always a presence in her life. As an aunt, she was still a great rememberer of birthdays and giver of welcome gifts. But she was obsessed with financial security. No one knew better than Agnes Macphail the problems of living on a very small government pension.

She had worked for many years to build the co-operative system, but when she applied for a job with the Ontario Co-operative Company, there was no opening for her. It seemed at times as if she were being rejected by the very people she had supported.

These setbacks, combined with the sense of being unwanted by the very people she had devoted her life to, made her more awkward in her dealings with others. She was offered a job in Ottawa but decided she didn't want to accept anything from the Liberals.

Some of her former colleagues were suggesting that she should be made a senator, but nothing was done to make it happen. When the bill to allow MPs a pension was finally passed, Agnes was one term short of being qualified to receive one. She was a sad woman at this time, short-tempered and difficult. She had been honoured and loved and now she was a back number.

"I had a letter returned from Ottawa," she told an audience, "I think it was yesterday, which said, 'Not known here.'"

Agnes was not feeling well, but she continued to make speeches, always trying to persuade her listeners to support the "party which cares for the people."

∞

In 1948, Agnes Macphail was elected to the Ontario Legislature again as the CCF member for York East. She had come to terms with being in a smaller chamber and to having fewer opponents. Her old enemy,

George Drew, had moved on to Ottawa to be leader of the Progressive Conservatives.

She kept on pressing for increased pensions and argued against rent control, which had been brought in during the war to prevent landlords from taking advantage of a shortage of housing. Her CCF colleagues were on the other side of the fence in that argument. They thought it was a necessary evil.

March 24, 1949, was Agnes's birthday. In the legislature that day she graciously accepted good wishes from E.B. Jolliffe and others. Leslie Frost, the provincial treasurer, had a special honour for her.

He stood up and said, "I would like to ask the Member for York East to present Bill number 12 on behalf of the House."

Bill #12 was a statement of welcome to Newfoundland on joining Confederation and becoming the tenth province.

Peace hadn't brought the good times expected by so many. The number of unemployed men and women grew, and life was hard in many parts of the country. Agnes was disturbed. She had seen it all before. "Are we going to go through the soup-bowl and flop-house regime again?" she asked.

She seconded a motion demanding equal pay for women doing equal work with men. "It is a straight case of justice," she told the members, pointing out that women worked as hard as men and for the same hours but for less money.

She sought legislation to continue the children's allowance to the age of eighteen and for more help for the disabled. She tried to get the means test abolished for pensioners. Tired and not well, struggling with her own problems, she never gave up on her many causes.

In the fall of 1951, Leslie Frost, now the premier of Ontario, introduced the Bill for extending the health service, for improvements in the welfare system of payments and other benefits. Agnes and the CCF had long fought for these measures, but Frost took all the credit himself. And in any case, Agnes Macphail was not satisfied. She said, "We will vote for it but it is not enough. I want to see...complete health service...medical care...hospital care, dental care, and whatever else they need."

This was to be her last speech as a representative of the people. In the provincial election that fall, only two members of the CCF were returned to the Ontario legislature. Agnes Macphail was not one of them.

∞

John Foote said he would get Agnes a post as Inspector of Women's Reformatories. She was delighted. Here was a job that might be not only a reward for all her work on prison reform but also an opportunity to continue to work on behalf of a group who needed help. She would have a decent salary again. She began to make plans.

Weeks passed and she heard nothing from Foote. She called and left messages, which were not

answered. At last he told her that he had been unable
to persuade the cabinet to give her the job. It was a terrible disappointment. It hit her like a final blow.

On her way to a dinner at which she was to be one
of the speakers, Agnes had another attack of cerebral
thrombosis. This was more serious than the last and
she never truly recovered from it.

∞

When she was feeling well again, she walked through
the city, looking wistfully in shoe-store windows at the
kind of shoes she had always loved to wear. Smart
leather shoes with heels and pointed toes. Now she had
to ask for flat, sensible ones because the last stroke had
weakened her sense of balance.

Once again worried about money, she tried to get
a variety of part-time jobs but wasn't really well enough
to work. She continued with her volunteer jobs for the
Elizabeth Fry Society and kept up with the affairs of
the CCF.

Agnes was well known to Canadians. Even those
who disagreed with her views saw her as a woman who
had forged her way ahead against much opposition and
who had fought bravely and tirelessly on behalf of others. Her supporters again pressed the prime minister
to award her a seat in the Senate, but again it wasn't
forthcoming. There was to be no easy money for Agnes
in these years.

But then she had a happy surprise. She bought a
lottery ticket from the boy who delivered her newspapers, and she won. The prize was a car. She already had

a car, so she took the cash – two thousand dollars – instead. Never forgetting the Party and her allegiance to it, she first made a large donation to the CCF. Some of the money went towards a payment on the mortgage. And she knew exactly what she was going to do with the rest.

"My name is Agnes Campbell Macphail," she said, "and I have never yet set foot in Scotland."

∞

She went off to find her roots. She and a friend crossed the Atlantic, not under sail as John and Jean Campbell had done, but in a modern liner, the *Empress of France*. The journey took not ten weeks but six days.

She went to Oban and found the countryside breathtakingly beautiful. Here were the lochs and glens Grandma Campbell had talked about so often. She walked on the rolling hills where Alexander Macphail, her grandfather, had helped his father tend the laird's sheep. In this green place, John Campbell had written his letter to the teacher and won a steel pen for it. He had forged his ambition in a schoolroom and so, in a sense, had his granddaughter.

She returned to Canada with a new feeling for the land of her forebears. She had loved every moment of her vacation even though the travelling had tired her out.

∞

Under pressure from people who pointed out her great contribution to the country, Prime Minister Louis

St. Laurent agreed at last to give Agnes Macphail a place in the Senate. He was to announce it later in the year.

She never did get to sit in that august chamber with its red plush-covered seats, a place she had, in any case, considered to be a retirement home for doddering old men. She had a heart attack and died in Wellesley Hospital, Toronto, on February 13, 1954.

There were many tributes, many fine things said about her in the newspapers and at her funeral service. Among the many floral tributes was a wreath from the Inmates Welfare Committee of Kingston Penitentiary. But perhaps what would have pleased Agnes most was the bust that was unveiled in the House of Commons the following year. Underneath her likeness there is a plaque which reads, "Agnes Campbell Macphail: First woman elected to the House of Commons, 1921–1940."

Agnes Campbell Macphail: A woman who made a difference.
Her image remains in the Parliament Buildings,
where she served with selfless devotion.

Chronology of Agnes Macphail (1890-1954)

Compiled by Lynne Bowen

MACPHAIL* AND HER TIMES	CANADA AND THE WORLD
1852	**1852**
John Campbell (Macphail's maternal grandfather) woos twenty-two-year-old Jean Black (Macphail's maternal grandmother), the orphaned daughter of a coal miner, away from his brother; they marry and leave Scotland for Canada West.	Immigration, mostly from the British Isles, has tripled and then doubled the population of Canada West (formerly Upper Canada) in the past twenty-seven years; 20 per cent of the immigrants are from Scotland.
1855	
Having worked at various jobs, the Campbells save enough money to buy land in Proton Township, Grey County; they settle near Alexander and Jean (née Jack) MacPhail, who had immigrated from Scotland with their parents.	

* Agnes Macphail changed the spelling of her family name from MacPhail to Macphail. For consistency, we have used her preferred spelling when referring to Agnes throughout this book.

MACPHAIL AND HER TIMES

CANADA AND THE WORLD

1857
Ottawa is chosen as the capital of the Province of Canada formed from the union of Upper and Lower Canada in 1841.

1864
Dougald MacPhail (Macphail's father) is born to Alexander and Jean MacPhail.

1867
British North America Act establishes the Dominion of Canada; Canada West becomes the province of Ontario.

Emily Stowe graduates from medical school in New York and after several years becomes the first Canadian woman to practise medicine.

1868
Emily Murphy née Ferguson (future magistrate and suffragette) is born in Cookstown, Ontario.

1872
The Grange is formed for the protection of Ontario farmers.

1873
Nellie McClung née Mooney (future reformer and author) is born at Chatsworth, Ontario.

1874
First Canadian branch of the Women's Christian Temperance

MACPHAIL AND HER TIMES

CANADA AND THE WORLD

Union (WCTU) originates in Owen Sound, Ontario.

1876
Dr. Emily Stowe founds the Toronto Women's Literary Club, Canada's first suffrage group.

1878
In Canada, Sir John A. Macdonald wins the federal election with the "National Policy," which favours industrialists over farmers and urban over rural constituents.

1885
The national WCTU is organized in Canada to campaign for Prohibition and to promote female suffrage, sex hygiene, and mothers' allowances.

1889
John and Jean Campbell's daughter Henrietta (Etta) marries Dougald MacPhail in a Presbyterian manse, although the Campbells are opposed to orthodox religion.

1889
Patrons of Industry become an activist group for Ontario farmers.

Emily Stowe is the first president of the Dominion Women's Enfranchisement Association.

1890
Agnes Campbell Macphail is born in a small log house in Proton Township on March 24.

1894
Patrons of Industry elect seventeen members in the Ontario election.

MACPHAIL AND HER TIMES	CANADA AND THE WORLD

1895
Macphail attends S.S. No. 4
Proton, a one-room school.

1896
In Canada, Wilfrid Laurier's
Liberals win the federal election;
Patrons of Industry candidates fail
to win any seats.

Thérèse Casgrain née Forget (future senator) is born in Montréal;
Charlotte Whitton (future feminist
and politician) is born at Renfrew,
Ontario.

1897
In addition to being a farmer,
Dougald MacPhail becomes an
auctioneer and a cattle dealer.

1897
The British Empire celebrates
Queen Victoria's Diamond Jubilee.

1899
World's first Peace Conference is
held in The Hague, in the
Netherlands.

1899-1902
Boer War is fought in South
Africa; Canada sends troops to
support Britain; the war divides
Canadians along French and
English lines.

1900
In Canada, most women who own
property are now allowed to vote
in municipal elections.

1901
Emily Murphy publishes *The
Impressions of Janey Canuck*.

MACPHAIL AND HER TIMES

1902
On the strength of Etta's inheritance, the MacPhails move to a new home near the hamlet of Ceylon, Ontario.

1906
After two years at home, Macphail persuades her parents to let her go to high school in Owen Sound.

1908
Macphail completes her junior matriculation in two years; she moves to Stratford to study for her senior matriculation and to attend teachers' college; she boards with her uncle and aunt.

CANADA AND THE WORLD

1902
Robert Gardiner (Macphail's future lover) comes to Canada from Scotland.

1903
In Britain, Emmeline Pankhurst founds the National Women's Social and Political Union.

1904
James S. Woodsworth, future leader of the Co-operative Commonwealth Federation (CCF), works with immigrant slum dwellers in Winnipeg.

1905
Grace MacInnis née Woodsworth (future politician) is born in Winnipeg.

1907
Chautauquas begin to tour North America providing evangelical religion, education, and entertainment.

1908
Sowing Seeds in Danny, a first novel by Canadian activist Nellie McClung, becomes a national bestseller.

MACPHAIL AND HER TIMES

1909
Her aunt's gift of a Bible leads Macphail to join the Reorganized Church of Jesus Christ of the Latter-day Saints, which she admires for its social conscience.

1910
Having been accepted for all five of the teaching positions she applies for, Macphail chooses Gowanlocks school near Port Elgin on Lake Huron.

Macphail is reprimanded by her parents for her extravagant gifts.

1911
Macphail resigns at the end of the school year and quickly finds another position in Bruce County at Kinloss; she boards with Sam Braden, whose general store is the venue for lively debates on Liberal and free trade issues.

1913
Suffering from tiredness and behaviour changes, Macphail is diagnosed with "inward goitre" and returns home to recuperate.

1914
Her health improved, Macphail goes to visit her aunt and uncle in Alberta; she finds a teaching job near Oyen, where she comes in contact with the UFA; a close call with death during a winter storm sends her back to Ontario and

CANADA AND THE WORLD

1909
United Farmers of Alberta (UFA) is established in Edmonton to further rural economic, social, and political issues.

1910
In Canada, the National Council of Women speaks out in favour of women's suffrage.

Bertrand Russell, British philosopher, mathematician, and social reformer, publishes the first volume of *Principia Mathematica*.

1911
Canadian prime minister, Sir Wilfrid Laurier, advocating free trade with the U.S., loses the federal election to Robert Borden.

In Britain, Liberal David Lloyd George introduces the National Health Insurance Act.

1913
British suffragettes demonstrate in London; Mrs. Pankhurst is jailed for inciting persons to place explosives.

1914
In Ontario, the first compulsory social insurance legislation in Canada, the Workmen's Compensation Act, is passed; the United Farmers of Ontario (UFO) unites the Grange, the Patrons of Industry, and a few small co-operatives.

MACPHAIL AND HER TIMES

teaching jobs in Boothville and Sharon in East Gwillimbury Township.

Macphail becomes engaged to Robert Tucker, a medical student, who enlists in the army and goes overseas; the relationship dies.

1917
Macphail catches the attention of the editor of the *Farmers' Sun*, who urges her to join the UFO.

CANADA AND THE WORLD

In Canada, a royal commission reports on the need for prison reform, but no action is taken; organized labour advocates equal pay for equal work.

Britain declares war on Germany; Canada is automatically at war.

1915
The Women's International League for Peace and Freedom is founded in The Hague, the Netherlands, by women wishing to end war for all time.

1916
In Canada, Manitoba passes the first mothers' allowance legislation in the country; Emily Murphy is appointed the first woman magistrate in the British Empire.

1917
In Canada, Ontario women are given the vote in provincial elections; two women are elected to the Alberta legislature; a national coalition government is formed in Canada pledged to enact conscription and votes for women, both controversial measures, which propel the UFO into political action.

In the October Revolution in Russia, the Bolshevik (later the Communist) Party seizes power.

MACPHAIL AND HER TIMES	CANADA AND THE WORLD
	1918 World War One ends; over eight million have died and twenty-one million have been wounded; a worldwide influenza epidemic kills almost twenty-two million people in two years. In Canada, all female citizens (except status Indians) are eligible to vote in federal elections. In Britain, women over thirty get the vote.
1919 Macphail is given her first opportunity to make a public speech; listeners cheer her ten-minute address loudly. During the Ontario provincial election campaign, Macphail is invited to speak at nomination meetings; the UFO wins forty-four seats and forms the government.	**1919** In Canada, Canadian women now can run in federal elections; when 30,000 Winnipeg workers leave their jobs in a general strike, federal troops occupy the city and arrest several labour leaders, including J.S. Woodsworth. The Peace Conference results in the Treaty of Versailles; the League of Nations meets in Paris. Lady Nancy Astor is the first woman elected to the British Parliament.
1920 While in Bowmanville to make a speech, Macphail falls ill with smallpox; her health restored, she begins to write a column for the *Farmers' Sun*.	**1920** In Canada, farmers from Ontario and the Prairies unite with dissident Liberals led by Thomas Crerar to form the Progressive Party. Canada joins the League of Nations; the U.S. does not.

MACPHAIL AND HER TIMES

Macphail refuses to accept a nomination in a federal by-election in North York.

Macphail is elected director of the North York United Farm Women; she addresses the annual UFO convention; she is appointed to the executive of the Women's Section of the Canadian Council of Agriculture.

1921
Macphail resigns her teaching position and goes home to nurse her Grandmother Campbell; she is nominated to be the UFO-Independent Labour candidate for South-East Grey over ten male nominees and refuses to step down when asked to at a second nomination meeting.

On December 6, Macphail is the first woman elected to the Canadian Parliament; the UFO affiliates itself with the Progressive Party, which has won sixty-five seats, the second largest number in Parliament, but refuses to act as the official Opposition.

1922
Macphail is sworn in as a Member of Parliament (MP); her maiden speech on March 27 addresses gender equality; she and the Progressives force a debate on working conditions at the Cape Breton mines.

CANADA AND THE WORLD

In the U.S., women are given the vote.

English writer, H.G. Wells, publishes *Outline of History*.

Unemployment insurance is introduced in Britain and Austria.

1921
In Canada, Liberal William Lyon Mackenzie King becomes prime minister; Nellie McClung is elected to the Alberta legislature; Irene Parlby (Alberta) and Mary Ellen Smith (British Columbia) become the first female cabinet ministers in the British Empire.

Conference on disarmament takes place in Washington, D.C.

1922
Union of Soviet Socialist Republics (U.S.S.R.) is formed from the former Russian empire.

Mussolini forms a fascist government in Italy.

MACPHAIL AND HER TIMES

Macphail embarks on the first of many speaking tours to the Prairie provinces.

As some Progressives, including Crerar, join the Liberals, Macphail struggles to remain nonpartisan.

1923
In her speech at the "No More War Rally" in Toronto, Macphail provides a listing of references to war in Ontario school texts.

When farm and labour candidates are defeated in the Ontario provincial election, the UFO abandons political activity; Macphail continues to believe that "co-operative government" is best.

1924
Macphail and nine others secede from the Progressive caucus and, with members of the Labour Party, form the "Ginger Group," which supports proportional representation, sexual equality, and prison reform.

At the Women's International League for Peace and Freedom meeting in Washington, D.C. Macphail makes contact with eminent women from other countries.

1925
Macphail changes the spelling of her family name from MacPhail.

CANADA AND THE WORLD

1923
In the U.S., Nevada and Montana introduce old-age pensions; New York opens the first birth control clinic in the country.

In Canada, inmates create a disturbance at Kingston penitentiary.

The Jazz Age is in full swing; George Gershwin composes "Rhapsody in Blue."

1924
First Labour government under Ramsay MacDonald in Britain is shortlived; Conservative Stanley Baldwin becomes prime minister; Winston Churchill crosses the floor to become Chancellor of the Exchequer.

Trades and Labour Congress of Canada drops its opposition to convict labour.

1925
In the Canadian general election on October 29, the Progessives elect only nine members, but they hold the balance of power since

MACPHAIL AND HER TIMES

Macphail travels to Glace Bay, Nova Scotia, to view firsthand the living conditions of coal mining families.

In campaigning for the general election, Macphail declares herself accountable only to the UFO and her constituents; after the election she works with a government committee on the Old Age Pensions Bill.

Macphail cancels a trip to Europe when Prime Minister King needs her vote to stay in power.

Macphail goes to Quebec to help Thérèse Casgrain in the fight for suffrage.

Although she has several suitors, Macphail remains single; her favourite forms of recreation are conversation and dancing.

1926
Macphail campaigns for UFO candidate Farquhar Oliver in the Ontario provincial election; he wins.

Macphail is finally successful at introducing legislation to allow convicts to work.

Mackenzie King asks for her support to defeat Meighen; in the federal election campaign that follows, Macphail is accused of being a Bolshevik; she wins her seat, but has nothing further to do with the Progressives.

CANADA AND THE WORLD

the Liberals need them in order to stay in power.

Unemployment Insurance Act is passed in Britain.

The Charleston is the fashionable dance.

1926
In Canada, Governor General Lord Byng refuses Prime Minister King's request in June that he dissolve Parliament; Byng appoints Conservative leader, Arthur Meighen, to be prime minister; three days later, on July 1, King's Liberals defeat Meighen's Conservatives by one vote.

The United Farmers of Canada (Saskatchewan Section) is established.

Imperial Conference issues the Balfour Declaration, which de-

Agnes Macphail

University of Toronto Women's Union declares during a debate that it would rather be Agnes Macphail than film star Mary Pickford.

clares that Britain and the Dominions are constitutionally equal in status.

1927

Insisting that the committee to organize celebrations for Canada's Diamond Jubilee include a representative of organized labour, Macphail agrees to serve as the sole MP.

In one of her regular newsletters to school children, Macphail questions British opium trade in China; she is forced to justify herself in the House.

1927

The motion picture "The Jazz Singer" is the first talkie; the slow foxtrot is the fashionable dance.

Charles Lindbergh flies his monoplane nonstop from New York to Paris.

1928

Always in need of money, Agnes does a ten-week speaking tour of western Canada with the Chautauqua shows.

1928

Supreme Court of Canada says that women cannot be senators because they are not "persons."

In Paris, Canada is among the first of the sixty-five nations that eventually sign the Kellogg-Briand Pact outlawing war.

1929

Macphail attends the International Women's League meeting in Prague, then the League of Nations meeting in Geneva; she asks to be assigned to work for disarmament instead of health and welfare.

Charles Baynes, a handsome, well-educated former inmate, offers to work with Macphail on prison reform.

1929

With the collapse of the U.S. Stock Exchange on October 28, the ten-year-long Great Depression begins.

MACPHAIL AND HER TIMES	CANADA AND THE WORLD
Macphail denounces Hugh Guthrie, a Conservative MP.	Alberta's "famous Five" (Emily Murphy, Henrietta Edwards, Louise McKinney, Nellie McClung, and Irene Parlby) petitions the Judicial Committee of the Privy Council, which reverses the Supreme Court of Canada's 1928 decision in the Persons Case.
1930 Dougald MacPhail dies. In the federal election, six women run but only Macphail is elected.	**1930** In Canada, the Conservatives under R.B. Bennett win the federal election; Hugh Guthrie becomes Minister of Justice; Cairine Wilson is the first woman appointed to the Senate. Britain, the U.S., France, Japan, and Italy sign a naval disarmament treaty.
1931 Macphail tours from head of the Great Lakes to Victoria speaking about arms reduction; she serves as vice-president of the Co-operative Union of Canada.	**1931** Statute of Westminster grants Canada full legal freedom from Britain except for amending the Constitution. Ontario farmers' incomes shrink by 50 per cent. The Women's International League for Peace and Freedom initiates a petition campaign for universal disarmament.
1932 Macphail, Woodsworth, and the Independent Group of MPs campaign for repeal of the Immigration Act, which allows police to quell legitimate dissent.	**1932** In Canada, Prime Minister Bennett insults union demonstrators by surrounding their Parliament Hill rally with policemen.

MACPHAIL AND HER TIMES

In the public uproar over conditions in prisons, Macphail proposes an investigation and becomes the centre of a national campaign to modernize the system.

Events in Ottawa prevent Macphail from being in Calgary when farmers' organizations, the Ginger Group, and the League for Social Reconstruction combine to found the Co-operative Commonwealth Federation (CCF).

1933
"A warring coalition of farmer, labour, and socialist organizations," the Ontario CCF chooses Macphail as its president.

Charles Baynes is arrested and charged with indecent assault; Macphail believes he is being persecuted; he is convicted but asks Macphail to help him avoid being sent to Kingston Penitentiary; her efforts on his behalf alert Minister of Justice Hugh Guthrie to her association with Baynes.

1934
Macphail presents a motion for prison reform; Guthrie reveals that

CANADA AND THE WORLD

Tim Buck, leader of the Communist Party of Canada, is jailed in the Kingston Penitentiary; riots at the Kingston and Stony Mountain penitentiaries focus public attention on the prison system.

First U.S. unemployment insurance law is enacted in Wisconsin.

1933
Franklin Roosevelt is sworn in as President of the U.S., proposes a "New Deal," and includes a woman in his cabinet.

The gross national product of Canada has declined by 42 per cent since the beginning of the Depression; 30 per cent of the work force is unemployed; the number of inmates in Canadian penitentiaries has increased 60 per cent in the past decade.

In Regina, the CCF chooses J.S. Woodsworth as leader.

Emily Murphy dies at Edmonton.

Adolf Hitler is appointed German Chancellor.

1934
U.S.S.R. joins the League of Nations.

MACPHAIL AND HER TIMES

Baynes is a homosexual with a criminal record; although Macphail is aware of his homosexuality and regards it as blameless, it is illegal under the Criminal Code.

The UFO leaves the CCF, forcing Macphail to leave too.

Macphail breaks off an affair with Robert Gardiner.

1935
Macphail undergoes surgery.

Macphail has herself locked in a punishment cell and challenges the right of the state "to deprive any living soul of light and air."

In the federal election, six women run but only two are elected; Macphail wins as a Farmer-Labour candidate in the riding of Grey-Bruce.

1936
Macphail visits Sweden, where she praises the social democratic government, and the Soviet Union, where she is not impressed with the results of communism.

Advertised as the "Lady Astor of Canada," Macphail joins Winston Churchill, Bertrand Russell, and H.G. Wells on American Harold Peat's list of eminent touring lecturers.

CANADA AND THE WORLD

Dionne quintuplets are born in Callendar, Ontario.

1935
Mackenzie King wins the Canadian election in a landslide; Justice Minister Earnest Lapointe appoints a royal commission headed by Joseph Archambault to investigate prison conditions.

Mussolini invades Abyssinia; the League of Nations declares Italy an aggressor and imposes sanctions.

1936
Spanish Civil War begins.

Mussolini and Hitler proclaim the Rome-Berlin Axis.

King George V dies and is succeeded by King Edward VIII, who abdicates in order to marry Wallis Simpson; they become the Duke and Duchess of Windsor; the new King is George VI.

Agnes Macphail

Macphail is sympathetic towards the romance of King Edward and Mrs. Simpson.

1937

When Ontario Premier Mitchell Hepburn sends special police ("Hepburn's Hussars") to rough-handle strikers at a General Motors plant in Oshawa, Macphail says, "Labour will organize and a little tinpot Mussolini like Hepburn will not stop it."

Macphail takes part in an international radio broadcast with Nancy Astor and U.S. congresswoman, Caroline O'Day.

Macphail interrupts a speaking tour to nurse her dying mother, Etta.

1938

Macphail begins to attend the CCF caucus; she promises to abide by its secrecy but reserves her right to dissent.

Archambault presents Macphail with a copy of his royal commission report with a special inscription.

1939

Although J.S. Woodsworth resigns as leader of the CCF rather than vote for Canada's entry into the war, Macphail reluctantly votes in favour.

1937

In Canada, the drought in southern Saskatchewan is the worst in its history; Quebec passes the Padlock Act, which can be used to evict communists; left-wing Canadians volunteer for the international brigades to assist the communist-supported republican government during the Spanish Civil War.

1938

Hitler marches into Austria; Britain tries to appease Germany at Munich.

1939

The Spanish Civil War ends; Britain and France recognize the new fascist government.

World War Two begins in September; Canada declares war on Germany and Italy.

MACPHAIL AND HER TIMES	CANADA AND THE WORLD
Macphail is a passenger on Trans-Canada Airlines' first cross-country flight.	A branch of the Elizabeth Fry Society begins service to female inmates in Vancouver.

In May, Macphail is presented to the King and Queen when they visit Canada to solidify support for the coming war.

1940

Campaigning on the Farmer-Labour ticket, Macphail loses her seat in the federal election; then she runs unsuccessfully for the United Reform Party in a Saskatoon by-election.

Macphail and the UFO help create the Farm Radio Forum, an experiment in adult education.

1940

In Canada, Quebec women are allowed to vote in provincial elections; the Liberals win a huge majority in the federal election; the Unemployment Insurance Act passes; the War Measures Act bans the Communist Party of Canada.

Winston Churchill becomes prime minister of Britain.

1941

Ineligible for a pension and in need of an income, Macphail undertakes several speaking engagements and agrees to write a column for the Globe entitled "Farm Betterment."

1941

CCF is the official opposition in British Columbia; Grace MacInnis is among those elected.

Japan bombs Pearl Harbor on December 7; U.S., Britain, and Canada declare war on Japan; the "Manhattan Project" (intensive atomic research) begins.

1942

A family tragedy prompts Macphail to move to Toronto with her two nieces; she rents a large house, hires two servants, and takes in boarders all the while continuing her work for civil liberties and adult education.

1942

In Canada, unaffiliated Progressives link with the Conservative Party to become the Progressive Conservative Party.

J.S. Woodsworth dies.

MACPHAIL AND HER TIMES

Macphail rejoins the CCF.

1943
Macphail runs in the Ontario election in York East for the CCF; she and Rae Luckock are the first women elected to the Ontario legislature; the CCF becomes the official Opposition.

1944
Macphail wages an ongoing battle with Conservative premier George Drew.

1945
Having kept the Archambault report on prison reform in the public eye for seven years, Macphail finally sees some of its recommendations put into effect.

Macphail suffers a slight stroke.

In the Ontario provincial election, the CCF loses all but eight seats; Macphail is defeated.

An inheritance from her former lover, Robert Gardiner, allows Macphail to travel to Mexico.

CANADA AND THE WORLD

U.S. and Canada forcibly move Japanese citizens inland away from the west coast of North America.

1943
Canadian Sir Harry Oakes, wealthy mining entrepreneur, is murdered in the Bahamas, where the Duke of Windsor is Governor.

1944
D-Day invasion by Allies on June 6 begins the liberation of Europe from the Nazis.

In response to the CCF victory in Saskatchewan, Prime Minister King introduces family allowances; a conscription crisis divides Canadians along French/English lines, but is less divisive than in World War One.

1945
Germany surrenders on May 8; the U.S. drops atomic bombs on Japan on August 6 and 9; Japan surrenders on September 2.

United Nations (U.N.) Charter is signed on June 26; Canada is one of the signatories.

Family allowances are introduced in Britain.

MACPHAIL AND HER TIMES

Women's suffrage becomes the law in France.

1948
Macphail runs in York East in the Ontario provincial election and wins; she is the only woman elected.

Macphail fights for equal pay for work of equal value.

1949
Macphail presents the bill welcoming Newfoundland into Confederation.

CCF in Ontario proposes the first pay equity legislation in Canada; Macphail seconds the bill; the legislation fails but a weaker version passes.

CANADA AND THE WORLD

1948
In Canada, the CCF regains its position as official Opposition in Ontario; Louis St. Laurent succeeds Mackenzie King as Liberal prime minister.

U.N. adopts the Universal Declaration of Human Rights, the first draft of which was written by Canadian John Humphrey.

1949
Newfoundland joins Confederation; Canada joins the North Atlantic Treaty Organization (NATO).

Communist Peoples' Republic of China is proclaimed.

The U.S.S.R. tests its first atom bomb.

1950
North Korea invades South Korea; U.N. forces land but are forced to withdraw.

1951
Nellie McClung dies at Victoria, B.C.

Charlotte Whitton is elected Canada's first woman mayor in Ottawa.

MACPHAIL AND HER TIMES

1951

After visiting an exemplary correctional centre for women in West Virginia, Macphail becomes honorary president of the new Toronto branch of the Elizabeth Fry Society.

In the Ontario election campaign, Grace MacInnis accompanies Macphail; the CCF and Macphail are defeated.

1952

Having suffered another stroke, Macphail recuperates and uses a $2000 prize to finance a visit to Scotland.

1953

Elizabeth Fry Society uses Macphail in its fund-raising campaign; she is acknowledged by the American Congress of Correction meeting in Toronto; she makes a brilliant speech at the CCF convention in November.

1954

Macphail works on a report about the status and welfare of women in Ontario.

She suffers a heart attack and dies in hospital on February 13 in Toronto.

A funeral and two memorial services precede Macphail's burial in the same Grey County graveyard as her parents.

CANADA AND THE WORLD

1952

King George VI dies and is succeeded by Queen Elizabeth II.

1953

Korean armistice is signed.

Hillary and Tenzing are the first to climb Mount Everest.

1954

U.S. and Canada agree to build the DEW (Distant Early Warning) line.

Senator Joseph McCarthy conducts televised witch hunt to prove Communist infiltration of the U.S.

Dr. Jonas Salk, developer of antipolio serum, begins to inoculate children.

Prime Minister Louis St. Laurent says he had intended to appoint Macphail to the Senate.

1955
A bust of Macphail is unveiled in Parliament.

1958
Ellen Fairclough becomes the first female cabinet minister in Canada.

Sources Consulted

The National Archives, Ottawa
The National Library, Ottawa

Books:

CLEVERDON, Catherine L. *The Woman Suffrage Movement in Canada*. Toronto: University of Toronto Press, 1950.

BOTHWELL, Robert, DRUMMOND, Ian, ENGLISH, John. *Canada 1900–1945*. Toronto: University of Toronto Press, 1987.

FRENCH, Doris and STEWART, Margaret. *Ask No Quarter*. Toronto: Longmans Green and Co., 1959.

MORTON, W.L. *The Progressive Party in Canada*. Toronto: University of Toronto Press, 1950.

Index

Anderson, Harry (reporter), 68, 74, 75
Archambault, Joseph (justice), 75, 76, 153, 154
Astor, Nancy, Viscountess (politician), 60, 146, 154

Balfour Declaration, 89, 149
Baynes, Charles (former prisoner), 68, 70-74, 111, 150, 152, 153
Bennett, Richard Bedford (politician), 49, 51, 69, 101-02, 103, 104, 105-06, 110, 151
Bolshevik revolution, 45, 145
Boothville, Ontario, 19, 144
Braden, Sam, 16, 24, 144
British North America Act (BNA), 55, 140
Buck, Tom (politician), 51, 152
Byng of Vimy, Julian Hedworth George, Viscount (Governor General), 37, 88, 149

Campbell, Jean Black (grandmother), 1-2, 3, 4, 6, 7, 8, 24, 29, 117, 136, 139, 141, 147
Campbell, John (grandfather), 3, 4, 6, 117, 136, 139, 141
Campbell, Ruby (friend), 131
Casgrain, Thérèse (senator), 54-55, 142, 149
Ceylon, Ontario, 2, 6, 9, 14, 17, 32, 34, 107, 116, 119, 123, 126, 131, 143
Chamberlain, Neville (politician), 118
Chautauqua, 95-97, 116, 143, 150

Church of Jesus Christ of Latter-day Saints (Mormon Church), 10, 30-31, 144
Churchill, Winston (politician), 116, 148, 153, 155
Communism, 51, 69, 71, 114-15, 129, 152, 154, 157
See also Bolshevik revolution
Conservative Party, 16, 25, 29, 30, 34, 35, 49, 69, 71, 75, 85, 86, 88, 89, 90, 91, 101, 102, 103, 110, 114, 125, 130, 149, 151
See also Progressive Conservative Party
Co-operative Commonwealth Federation (CCF), 49-51, 55, 105, 107, 110, 121, 125, 126, 129-31, 132, 133, 134, 135, 136, 152, 153, 154, 155, 156, 157, 158
See also Macphail, Agnes, and the CCF
Co-operative movement, 48, 132, 148, 151
Coote, George (politican), 39
Craig, R.W. (commission member)
Crerar, Honourable Thomas Alexander (politician), 34, 39, 48, 146, 148
Customs scandal, 86, 87-88

Depression. *See* Great Depression
Diamond Jubilee of Canada committee, 98
Dominion Women's Enfranchisement Association. *See* Women's suffrage.
Drew, George (politician), 130, 131, 133, 156
Drought. *See* Great Depression

*Printed in May 2000
at Marc Veilleux Imprimeur Inc.,
Boucherville (Québec).*